Thon

WITHIN OUR GRASP

CHANGING OURSELVES
and the
WORLD

a memoir

First U.S. Edition, 2024

ISBN: 979-8-9906886-0-5 (pbk)
ISBN: 979-8-9906886-1-2 (ebk)

Book design by Christina Thiele, CreateForGood
Editorial and self-publishing guidance by Spoonbridge Press

Printed in the U.S.A.

TRAILBLAZER™
PUBLISHING LLC

To my grandchildren

Contents

Introduction

At precisely 8:46 a.m. on the eleventh of September, 2001, as the sun cast its golden rays upon the bustling metropolis of New York City, the serene stillness was shattered by a deafening roar. With a chilling precision, American Airlines Flight 11 pierced the majestic North Tower of the renowned World Trade Center. The impact unleashed an inferno of chaos and destruction. A cascade of shattered glass and twisted steel rained down on the streets below, sending shockwaves of terror through the hearts of onlookers and reverberating across the globe. This was the first of four related attacks that morning, now commonly referred to as the 9/11 attacks.

My wife Phyllis and I lost our twenty-five-year-old niece, Katie McCloskey, that morning; our children, Kristen, Katie, and Mark, lost their cousin. Katie McCloskey was like a daughter to Phyllis and me, and our children loved her like a sister. She was so young, with her whole life ahead of her; her death was gruesome, tragic, and traumatizing. That day my family lost its innocence and was forced to face the horrors of terrorism. To this day, I cannot erase the mental images of the planes flying into the buildings.

Five months later, Phyllis, our twin daughters, and I visited Ground Zero, the site where the World Trade Center had formerly stood, and where Katie McCloskey had worked and died. The area was an immense, expansive crater, with the surrounding buildings scorched black and with windows missing or shattered. It reminded me of a war zone. Ten years after that, Phyllis, Kristen, Katie, Mark, and I would attend the dedication ceremony of the 9/11 Memorial, and I was grateful when our country memorialized those lost that day.

My family considers that sacred ground—our beloved Katie's final resting place.

How I looked at life changed forever when my niece died that day. While many Americans sought retribution—on September 14, 2001, Congress authorized military retaliation against Al Qaeda and its Taliban enablers in Afghanistan, with only one lawmaker voting against it—my thinking was on a different path. I began my quest for meaning in the face of this tragedy.

I wanted to learn more about why the men had hijacked those planes on 9/11 to cause so much destruction, death, and suffering. What led them to resort to this violent action? Compelled to find the answers, I yearned to determine the root cause. And I began to wonder, *What can I do to contribute to a more peaceful world in the future, to prevent another 9/11 from happening?*

God's presence enveloped me from the outset of this miraculous journey. I opened my heart and allowed myself to be led by the spirit. My niece Katie appeared to me in a dream within a week of her death, and her words comforted me. She became my Angel Katie at that moment, and Angel Katie has continued to connect with me from that point forward, to the present day.

Searching for meaningful direction for the next five years after 9/11, I traveled three times to Rhinebeck, New York, to attend workshops at the Omega Institute for Holistic Studies. There were three main takeaways from those workshops: that we as human beings can develop non-violent relationships by listening to one another, developing empathy, and building trust and respect; how important it is to live the second part of your life with purpose, finding your passion and leaving a legacy; and that I needed to trust myself, follow my intuition and insight, and allow myself to be led and guided.

These three takeaways would be amplified in December 2006,

when I attended a graduation ceremony at LaRoche College, a small liberal-arts college in Pittsburgh with a global perspective. The keynote speaker, who was an alumnus of the Fletcher School—a Tufts University graduate school—spoke on global issues, focusing on global peace. Her speech was the spark that ignited my passion.

When Phyllis and I returned home that evening, already aware that the Fletcher School was a world-renowned graduate school of international relations, I scurried up the stairs to my home-office computer to check out its website. I was pleased to discover that the Fletcher School offered a mid-career program that seemed ideal for my needs. My heart said yes. But my brain said no—largely because of the $62,500 price tag.

That tuition cost brought a lot of trepidation. Just the thought of it triggered memories of an adolescent trauma, when my father's business failed and my family abruptly became poor. My sense of safety and security had evaporated overnight—and the experience had left an everlasting scar.

It took me eighteen months to work through my fear of taking on such an enormous undertaking and expense at my stage of life. I consulted with Phyllis and with other members of my family, as well as with friends, mentors, and spiritual advisors. I moved cautiously forward, and eventually found the courage to apply for admission. I was placed on a waiting list for a year, and in May of 2009, I gained admission into the Fletcher School. At nearly fifty-five, I was the oldest student in my class.

I proceeded with this plan despite my wife's concerns and objections. It was the first time in our thirty-two years of marriage that we did not find a resolution to a dispute. Phyllis was furious, and how could I blame her? I would be taking on a significant amount of debt while we were still paying off our children's college loans—and I had no concrete plan of what I was going to accomplish by this expensive and time-consuming undertaking. Our marriage was challenged as it had never been before, and it would be a source of discord for the next decade of our life together.

Phyllis thought I had gone crazy, and surely there was some craziness going on: God was meddling in my life. Phyllis had often teased me about being insanely optimistic, trusting, and naïve, but this time I had pushed the envelope. Never had I acted on a wing and a prayer, but I now took a leap of faith, inspired by a force beyond my control.

I found a portal to a whole new world on that first day of class at the Fletcher School. With classmates from all over the world, it felt as if I was sitting in the General Assembly at the United Nations. I was surrounded by exceptional students united by a common trait: open-mindedness combined with intellectual curiosity.

My Fletcher School experience would ultimately broaden my mind, introduce me to a global peace building community, and lead me down an altruistic path. I faced challenges: I had not been in school for thirty-two years, for example, and technology had changed a lot since. But I found the vision I was seeking early in the first term, when one of our professors discussed diplomacy at the grassroots, or local community, level. This, I believed, was something I could do.

I would go on to learn about the Contact Theory, a central tenet of peace-building. This is a theory of change that emphasizes intergroup contact and the development of personal relationships on a more intimate level, to break down stereotyping and prejudice and enemy images. I would see that the organizations I researched while writing my thesis were providing an antidote to hatred, fear, and violent dehumanizing behavior by teaching youth and children how to get to know each other as human beings across ethnic, cultural, and religious differences.

And I realized I too could make a difference. I could create a charitable organization—a public foundation, global in scope—to help create awareness all over the world and raise money to support these global grassroots peace building efforts. I experienced a vision of the real possibility of how individual transformations can have a "ripple effect" on peace in the world.

My thesis became the cornerstone of the Global Peace Building Foundation (GPBF), which I founded six weeks after I completed my studies at the Fletcher School. Our date of incorporation was September 11, 2010—nine years after my niece Katie's death. The organization's mission is to "contribute to the building of global peace by supporting organizations and projects that restore, rebuild, and transform relationships that have been broken due to prejudices, stereotyping, hatreds, and fears that may have accumulated over generations."

This book is the story of the journey I took to find my path, to manifest my voice. And if there is anything that journey has taught me, it is that anyone can undertake it for themselves. You, too, can overcome your fear, release the burden that is holding you back, step out from your isolation and frustration, follow your passion, and discover your unique voice.

———

We learn as we go along in life, and our life experiences shape us. I was blessed with so many angels throughout my life: teachers, coaches, mentors, spiritual advisors, and role models all unselfishly provided me with guidance and encouragement. Their stories are forever embedded in my story, and in my heart. They lifted me up when I was down; they instilled a desire in me to help others, just as they'd helped me. These collective experiences over five decades provided me with a solid toolkit to launch the GPBF, and begin to help building peace in the world.

My GPBF journey has provided me with a breadth of learning experiences. My adolescent years were a walk in the park compared to the suffering and trauma experienced by too many of the world's youth and children. Like so many things in life, especially peace building, that is something we must see to believe. My belief in community has been reinforced too, along with the critical role of mentors, coaches, and teachers. I've learned that pure altruism has no strings attached; that volunteerism brings happiness and purpose; that little things can turn into big things.

Most importantly, I've learned that all of us, as ordinary citizens of the world, individually have the power to change the world. It is within our grasp. Whatever difference you want to make is possible. Offer your time and talents in ways that best speak to you. You can play an important role in making the world a better place.

Of course, change takes a long time, and the results may be intangible and difficult to measure. But you cannot quantify how human encounters and human experiences transform each of us. The peace-building leaders running the GPBF grantee organizations serve as a testament to this. They are in it for the long haul, because they see young people transformed by their programs. This, in turn, continues to inspire me. And I hope it will inspire you as well.

———

There are a few existential questions I feel we must ask ourselves, in order to live a meaningful life. How do we want to be remembered? What will be our legacy? Will it simply be career accomplishments and accumulated wealth? Or will we be remembered for our time commitments to others, for having nurtured our relationships, and for the meaningful contributions we made to our community and the world at large?

Future generations will be affected by what we do now—not only our children, grandchildren, and great grandchildren, but future generations of the children of the world. Think about that: it is an awesome responsibility, but with our hearts and minds in the right place, we are more than capable of living up to it.

———

PART 1

Nothing that can be said can begin to take away the anguish and the pain of these moments. Grief is the price we pay for love.

—QUEEN ELIZABETH II, IN SUPPORT OF THOSE WHO HAD
LOST LOVED ONES ON 9/11

CHAPTER ONE
An Awakening to the Spirit

I t was a typical Monday morning on my business-ownership treadmill. My mind was busy, but I wasn't getting anywhere. I was going to be heading to a fundraising golf event, but I was worried about money. Did I have enough work? Were there enough projects in the pipeline? Was I doing enough to build my practice? Were my clients satisfied with my work? Would I have enough cash to pay our real-estate taxes at the end of September? I kept telling myself, *I know it's hard to be on my own. But this is what I want. It's the cost of freedom.* As the sole income provider for my family, I felt the weight of the world on my shoulders. I was determined not to let them down.

Kristen and Katie, our identical twin daughters, had just started at Westminster College, around ninety minutes north of our home in Mt. Lebanon, Pennsylvania. My wife Phyllis was still very sad that her girls had grown up and were living away at college, and had cried every day for a while after we'd gotten them settled into their dorms. Meanwhile, our son Mark had just started his freshman year in high school. It was one of those transition periods that makes you aware of the passage of time.

I played golf that afternoon in the Lupus Challenge, an annual fundraising event founded by my good friend Tom Miller. The event was in honor of Tom's late wife, Kathleen Rooney Miller, who had died from lupus fourteen years earlier. When Phyllis and I got married, Kathleen was a bridesmaid and Tom a groomsman. The two of them were married a little over a year later, on October 21, 1978—six years to the day after I'd first met Phyllis and Kathleen at my dad's teenage dance hall.

The Lupus Challenge event would ultimately raise more than two million dollars over twenty-eight years for the Lupus Foundation of Pennsylvania, whose mission was to promote awareness, education, service, and research. That afternoon, the weather was sunny and cool, just perfect for the golf event—a casual round of golf topped off with a cocktail hour, delicious dinner, and raffle prizes.

Steve "Mac" McGinnis and I had been basketball teammates at Bethel Park High School, and had kept in touch since our high-school and college days. He and I inevitably wound up in the same foursome at the annual Lupus Challenge, and this day was no different. Our group also included our friend Kerry McCann, Mac's college roommate and fraternity brother at Bethany College, who was now an attorney. (Kerry and I were such terrible golfers, we always paired together on this golf outing. No one else wanted to play with us.) My friend since grade school, Frank Del Percio—who was a much better golfer than all of us—rounded out the foursome. But as a group, we were pretty bad. That year, we would win the award for having the worst score!

After the dinner, Tom gave a poignant speech about his wife, and his words prompted me to think about Kathleen and her perseverance, strength, hope, and deep faith while I drove home that evening.

In her college days at Bethany College, Kathleen had always seemed to be tired, and her lupus had remained undiagnosed until very late in her life. I had visited her in the hospital several weeks before she'd died. By then it was a normal routine for Kathleen to be in the hospital at somewhat regular intervals, but she'd always bounced back and returned home. I'd left work to visit her on three separate occasions while she was at Mercy Hospital, located near Duquesne University's campus in downtown Pittsburgh. It was hot and humid then, and Kathleen had tried to talk me out of coming to visit her in the sweltering heat. But I had gone anyway, though I kept my visits brief because of her fatigue.

My final visit, the last time I saw Kathleen, had been different. She was very weak. She asked me to hold her hand as she got out of bed, and to help her walk over to the window. She needed my help to keep her balance, and she dragged her feet; it became obvious that she hardly had enough strength to walk across the room to get to the window. As we looked outside, Kathleen told me that she was seeing double. This was rare—Kathleen ordinarily never talked about herself or gave in to self-pity, no matter how badly she felt.

She'd quickly switched to another subject, offering me some chocolates from "Grandfather." Her grandfather was Arthur J. Rooney, the founding owner of the Pittsburgh Steelers. She always referred to him as *Grandfather*, never *my grandfather*, which always amused me. I smiled once again. The fact that "Grandfather" had sent her a box of chocolates didn't surprise me; he had a reputation for doing kind things.

I'd kissed her goodbye and told her I loved her. As I left, I'd said, "I will be back soon"—and I went back to work. The thought had never entered my mind that that was the last time I would see Kathleen.

Phyllis had called me at work when Kathleen died. It had been a Saturday afternoon, and I was working in my office in Lawrenceville, a section of Pittsburgh. I'd immediately dropped what I was doing and raced home. When I'd gotten home, Phyllis and I had sat down on our bed, hugged each other, and both started to cry. Our girls, Kristen and Katie, didn't understand what was going on. They were only four and a half and had never seen me cry before. After looking puzzled, they'd jumped up on the bed and joined in on the hug, trying to comfort us.

It was at the funeral home, the morning of Kathleen's burial, when Tom had told me that there must have been a reason why I'd made those visits to see Kathleen while she was in the hospital, just prior to her death. Tom was grief-stricken, his face stark white. He sat in a chair by himself, and I walked over and stood next to him. I put my hand on his shoulder and began to cry. Kathleen's younger brother Jimmy walked over to us and tried to console me.

At Kathleen's funeral mass, held at Saint Peter Catholic Church on the Northside of Pittsburgh, I'd wept uncontrollably. Tears streamed down my face as I took communion. Father Mark Glasgow, of whom Kathleen had been fond, said, during the mass, that *"Kathleen's spirit will always remain with us."* His words have always stuck with me, and brought me great comfort as I experienced my first tragic death of a loved one. Kathleen had been only thirty-one when she died. Caitlin, Tom and Kathleen's daughter, was only a year old when her mother passed.

Little did I know how deeply Father Glasgow's words would resonate with me fourteen years later, the morning after we honored Kathleen on that sunny day in September—as the spirit of my niece Katie would lift me up in the face of the horrific events that were about to unfold.

CHAPTER TWO

Terrorism Hits Home

found September 11, 2001, another beautiful sunny morning, just like the day before, as I set out from home to meet Chas, my friend and client, and his attorney. We met in a conference room I shared with a local law firm, and soon after our meeting began, we heard people shouting. Our meeting was interrupted when an attorney stormed into the conference room to grab a television that was stored in the cabinet.

"Two planes just flew into the twin towers in New York City!" he shouted.

We became frozen for a few seconds, and looked at each other. Suddenly what we were talking about had become unimportant.

Chas broke the silence, announcing, "This meeting is over." We packed up our papers and headed out the door. As Chas and I walked out onto the sidewalk, it hit me. Cars were passing by on the busy road but suddenly I could not hear them. I turned to Chas.

"Oh my God, my niece works there!" I said.

Overcome with fear, I started to shake. I said goodbye to Chas, who told me he was going to church to pray. My first thought was that I had to get home to see if Phyllis knew what had happened.

As I drove out of the parking lot, I tuned in to NPR on the radio. The media was already saying that this was a terrorist attack, with mass casualties expected. I began to hope that somehow, some way, Katie had been able to escape the carnage. Maybe she was late getting to work. Maybe she didn't work that day. I prayed that she would be okay.

Katie had been almost two when Phyllis and I were married, and we had watched her grow up. We'd frequently traveled to South Bend, Indiana, to visit her parents, Phyllis' brother and sister-in-law Dick and Anne, and their kids, and the family were frequent visitors to Pittsburgh. The McCloskey kids—Leslie, Noah, Katie, and Julie—had been absolutely thrilled when their cousins were born, and the six to seven hours' drive between South Bend and Pittsburgh hadn't stopped our two families from becoming very close.

When I arrived home, it was eerily quiet. The only sound I heard was the *tick tock* of the grandfather clock. I ran up the stairs to my home office on the third floor, expecting Phyllis to be distraught. When I found her I shouted, "Is Katie okay?" She looked startled and confused—she had not yet heard the news.

Phyllis immediately telephoned Dick and Anne. I stood next to Phyllis and braced myself for their reaction. As soon as I heard Dick's voice, I knew it was bad. Dick was normally soft-spoken and unemotional; now he was crying, shouting. He said he couldn't get through to Katie. All the phones were down. At that moment I felt that everything was out of control. It was total chaos.

Phyllis and I went downstairs to the living room to watch the news coverage. We saw the planes flying into the buildings, another plane hitting the Pentagon. Then we heard about the plane that had crashed close to Pittsburgh. We were under attack. We sat there in disbelief, worried for our children's safety.

Our daughters called us from Westminster College, and we told them Katie was missing. We drove over to the high school and brought Mark home early. We telephoned Dick and Anne repeatedly into the evening. Phyllis stayed glued to the television. I sought refuge in my office. I couldn't work, though I called some of my clients. I kept going downstairs to check in with Phyllis. I felt numb.

Phyllis and I held each other close that night. We wondered if Katie was still alive—if somehow, she might be miraculously rescued by the first responders. But I felt as though Phyllis and I were at the bottom of a heap of concrete, rubble, and debris ourselves. We couldn't move. We couldn't escape.

It seemed as if we were the ones waiting to die.

———

CHAPTER THREE
Harsh Reality Sets In

By the next day, there was still no word on Katie. We saw reports on the television that no one was coming out alive. I could not get out of my mind the images of the planes flying into the buildings, which was replayed repeatedly on television. I couldn't escape them.

Bad news spreads quickly. Tom Miller called. While we were speaking, Tom must have glanced at the local Pittsburgh newspaper, and he interrupted me: "Oh my God, Waldie was on the first hijacked plane ... I have to call Mac!" I didn't make the connection at the time ... but later we would find out that our high-school friend Ken Waldie had been on the plane that flew into the WTC's North Tower, very close to where Katie worked.

Ken Waldie had gone to high school with Mac and me, and they had stayed close. Ken and I had grown up in the same neighborhood; he and I had often talked on the school bus. We shared the same interests in sports; he was a gifted student and swimmer. What I remembered most about him was his humility.

Our church held a special service in the chapel on Wednesday evening. At the end of the service, Phyllis shared that our niece was most likely killed. She asked for the congregation's prayers and wept. A church member walked over to Phyllis and hugged her; soon several other church members surrounded us to console us. Our pastor said a special prayer.

Dick called when we returned from church that evening. He and Katie's siblings had gathered Katie's toothbrush, her hairbrush, anything with a possible trace of her DNA, and were heading out to New York that evening. They would drive through the night and arrive at sunrise on Thursday morning.

Dick and the kids were among the many people who carried photos to the city in search of their loved ones. And Dick saw the goodness of humanity in what was happening at Ground Zero during those very dark days immediately after 9/11, with volunteers offering to stand in line for them as they waited for five hours at the Armory—which was the area's makeshift morgue—and offering them food, lodging, and cell phones.

There must have seemed something special about Dick and his kids as they walked about in search of Katie. My daughters and I were by the television in my bedroom when Dick suddenly appeared on television, on ABC evening news. He looked exhausted and distressed, and broke down in tears in the middle of the interview. I felt his suffering, and my heart went out to him. He explained that he and his family were from the Midwest, and that he had assumed the people of New York City were pushy and unfriendly. But he couldn't say enough good things about the people of this city.

Dick and his family returned home on Sunday, September 16, after visiting more than forty hospitals and the several armories. When they returned home, they said good things about the outpouring of support and goodwill they'd received from all the volunteers in New York City. What a blessing that was to us all.

But the grim reality was setting in. Katie would not be coming home.

CHAPTER FOUR
Remembering Katie

Kristen, Katie, Mark, and I arrived in South Bend around 5:00 p.m. on the evening of Wednesday, September 19, several days after Phyllis had driven there. It had been a solemn drive from Pittsburgh—a significant contrast to the many drives we'd made over the years in anticipation of boat rides on Lake Michigan, Notre Dame football games, golf outings, water skiing, and days and nights at the cottage on Indian Lake. When we pulled up to the house, I took a deep breath and said to the kids, "This isn't going to be easy."

We walked through the garage and entered the house through the pantry door into the kitchen. Anne greeted me with a big smile and said in her sweet voice, "Oh, Tommy, I am so glad you're here. Katie loved you so much." She and I began to weep as we hugged each other and she said, "We will never see her again." Dick came over and we hugged. He also told me how much he appreciated me being there as we cried together.

We were warmly greeted by all the rest of the South Bend McCloskey family. Phyllis's brothers, Mark and David, and sister-in-law, Laverna, had flown in from New Mexico. Dick and Betty McCloskey had flown in from Florida. We all gathered to support each other, and there was a steady stream of friends and neighbors stopping by the house bringing food and offering their condolences that evening.

The next morning while I was waking up, just as the sun was

rising and the birds chirping, Katie came to me in a dream, vivid and real. She said to me in her soft voice, "Uncle Tom, please don't worry. I am okay." It warmed and comforted me, as if Angel Katie had appeared to put my mind at ease.

Friends and neighbors stopped by the house all day. Dick and I went over to the Notre Dame campus to preview a professionally produced video of Katie's life to be broadcast on television, before and after her memorial service. The video brought both happy and sad emotions; Anne cried every time she saw it.

On Thursday afternoon, we gathered in the den and shared stories about Katie. I told about when she had been learning to ride a bicycle—she didn't know how to brake, so she would just crash into something to stop. I also told the group that when our families had celebrated the millennium together in the Bahamas, several months previously, Katie had gazed into my eyes with her beautiful green ones, and whispered to me, "Uncle Tom, you are my favorite uncle."

Friday, the day of the memorial service, arrived quickly. I had never experienced anything like this before in my life, and I certainly wasn't alone. Before we left the house, Dick said to me, with tears in his

Who Was Katie McCloskey?

Katie McCloskey lived her life like most people wish they could, fearlessly and boldly. In twenty-five years, she achieved more of her goals and dreams than many accomplish in a lifetime.

"It was always her dream to go out and work in the Big Apple, as she called it," says my cousin Mark, her cousin. "That's something I always hold onto, that she had an opportunity to go out and live that big dream."

After graduating from Indiana University, Katie moved to New York City in March 2001 to live with her best friend Cherese. She didn't have a job yet, but she knew she wanted to leave the tiny town of South Bend, and so she did.

Katie packed up her life and her Lhasa Apso, Spencer, and drove off in her red Mustang convertible to start life in New York City.

"Her favorite color was red, so of course she got a red car," says my daughter Kristen, laughing. "Last time I saw her in person was her driving back to New York City in June after our graduation party. I just remember her driving away from our party and waving from her red convertible."

Even as a child, Katie had never seemed to question her desires. Despite being allergic to several different foods, she never let it stop her from living her life.

"I can remember her going into anaphylactic shock like two or three times growing up...she would just brush it off," says Kristen. "Katie had the most bubbly, carefree personality I've ever met. She was so, so, *so* funny. Even though she was clumsy—she'd trip over or run into things—she'd laugh it off."

After a month of job hunting, Katie landed her dream job in New York City, working at the computer help desk of eyes, "I don't know if I can get through this." The memorial service was at St. Pius X Catholic Church, and it was packed. Dick, Anne, and their family sat in the front row in the center of the church, with our family behind them. Kristen and Katie sat next to me, and I held their hands during the entire service. We squeezed tight at moments when we just couldn't bear the pain. I saw Dick and Anne buckle over several times during the service.

I heard Katie's sister Leslie weep loudly when Katie's boyfriend began the eulogy: "Good afternoon. For those of you who don't already know me, my name is Richie Hayes, and Katie is the love of my life." Richie encouraged those in attendance to live as fully as Katie had. "Announce your goals and reach for them, just like Katie. Live life to the fullest, just like Katie. Laugh loudly and make others laugh, just like Katie. When you need a little inspiration, just close your eyes and remember Katie."

———

We headed home to Pittsburgh on Sunday. I realized the moment I pulled away from the curb that a major shift was occurring. We were leaving a bubble that felt safe and secure. Our family had faced the horror of terrorism

Marsh McLennan on the 97th floor of One World Trade Center. "She would send us pictures in the mail of her and her co-workers having rubber band fights at her desk...she loved her job," says Kristen.

Katie worked at the World Trade Center two to three days a week and waitressed at the WWF Restaurant in Times Square to help make ends meet. Even with two jobs, Katie still had the vigor to do the things she loved outside work. "I remember thinking to myself, *I'm exhausted, and I'm just in college...Katie works two jobs in New York City, travels in from Mount Vernon* [a 45-minute train commute], *and then goes out at night,*" Kristen recalls. "She just had so much energy for life...I feel like she really did just live for each moment. She was very present."

As a family, the McCloskeys and Etzels were incredibly close. We would visit each other three or four times a year, more often than most families who live a six-hour drive apart. We'd spend holidays together at the family lake house, play on the beach, or just lounge on the dock together.

"I remember sitting on a dock with her at the lake house and just feeling the sun hit our skin," says Kristen. "She would say stuff like, 'I'm so glad you're my cousin...I love you so much'—and she really meant it. Katie was a great sounding board for everything. We could talk to her about any trials going on in life, any friendship issues, drugs, sex...all the pivotal things you have questions about in middle school and high school."

Even while thriving in her new big-city life, Katie would always make time for her cousins. She'd call Kristen and Katie, in college at the time, to head-on, and we would never be the same.

It was the loss of innocence that struck me the most, as if we were venturing into a scary unknown. It was somewhat like when I had left my very small grade school thirty years before and was facing going to a large unfamiliar, public high school. Frankly, I was afraid—and on top of that, I was worried about how this trauma would affect my children for the rest of their lives.

But I had learned one important thing about loss and grief up to that point in my life, and from our friend Kathleen's death. *Your loved one who has passed away remains with you in spirit.*

check in and make sure they were acclimating well.

Katie loved her job and the budding life she was making in New York City, and with a view of the Statue of Liberty from her office, she really felt like she had made it. She was just living another day in her life when she went into work at the World Trade Center on September 11, 2001.

Her life, and more importantly her character, have left their mark on the family she leaves behind.

"There's been a lot born from that moment that no one expected," says Mark. "A lot of good. I didn't realize it back then, but it really impacted me spiritually and emotionally to leave the world better than I found it... Everything I do, I try and steer my energy back into love."

Kristen makes a point to wear red, Katie's favorite color, on 9/11 in Katie's honor. She's also tried to adopt Katie's passion for life and encourages her own family to live the same way.

A little less than a year before she died, on Thanksgiving Day in 2000, Katie documented her life's motto in one of her many letters and notes to Kristen:

This is Katie M. Kristen—you crack my shit up!!! You remind me a lot of myself in many ways ☺. My advice to you is simple, but VERY IMPORTANT!! Stay true to yourself. Never regret anything you do, because life is full of learning experiences. You learn from the mistakes you make. So make a lot of them! ☺ Also...cherish every day. Life is short, so don't take anything for granted. We are so lucky to be a part of such a loving family. I love you very much. Come visit me frequently! Love, Katie.

CHAPTER FIVE
The Aftermath

After every tragedy, things change—but some things go on. The Thanksgiving after 9/11, we had a huge gathering at our home with all the McCloskeys. There were so many of us that we couldn't all fit at our dining-room table. We borrowed a couple of long tables from our church and put them in the living room and dining room, transforming the first floor of our house into a makeshift dining hall.

Before dinner, we all took turns giving thanks. Several mentioned how important it was to provide support for each other. It was different not having Katie there with us. I remembered the year before when we'd watched the movie *Office Space*; Katie had said the movie was like her work. We howled laughing and exchanged "skritchies" (a mixture of backrubs and tickles), a McCloskey/Etzel family tradition.

Several of Kristen and Katie's high-school friends stopped over after dinner, and a few of us stood together by the bright, crackling fireplace. The noise of the crowd was just like what I remembered from when I was a disc jockey, playing records at my dad's crowded teenage dance hall in the '70s. It was magical.

The next day, the day after Thanksgiving, I did something I'd vowed I would never do: get a tattoo. Katie had had a tattoo in the shape of a sunfish on her stomach, and Phyllis came up with the idea of our getting a similar one in remembrance of her. She called around, and the owner of a shop on the South Side of Pittsburgh was willing to close her shop to the public on Friday afternoon so that all twelve of us could get the tattoo. Kristen drew a replica of Katie's tattoo as a guide.

I knew I was in trouble when the tattoo artist gave me a tennis ball to squeeze. I asked her, "What's this for?" and she laughed and told me, "You'll figure it out." I never stopped squeezing it the whole time.

My tattoo is in the shape of a sunfish, like Katie's: red, white, and blue, with *Katie* encircled by its yellow halo. Katie would have been proud of me stepping out of my comfort zone—for her.

A revelation came to me as the artist was wrapping up: *Angel Katie is present and watching over me.* My tattoo was an in-the-flesh reminder that Angel Katie would remain with me as long as I am alive on this earth—until she and I are reunited in heaven.

It was worth it.

———

Toward the middle of January, Dick and Anne informed us that they were going to New York City to visit Ground Zero. At the time, we hesitated; we weren't certain we could handle it.

But on the evening of Friday, February 22, Phyllis and I drove to Westminster College to pick up Kristen and Katie. We'd decided we would visit the city that weekend, and Ground Zero on Sunday. We felt it was time for us to be there—to face up to our deep sadness, an important step in our healing.

Mark stayed back, having decided it was too much for him, but Phyllis, Kristen, Katie, and I left for the city early Saturday morning. We deliberately made it an adventure—very much out of character for me. We didn't make hotel reservations or any route plans; we just drove. We randomly chose a turnpike exit to Jersey City that seemed the right way to go. I asked the turnpike attendant if we were going in the correct direction. He said it was, and told us that the exit would conveniently take us to a Marriott Hotel. It turned out that this hotel was perfect for us—it was super easy to park there and walk the short distance to the train that would take us directly into Manhattan.

I had been to New York a few times before this trip. Phyllis, Dick, Anne, and I had visited Leslie when she was in medical school there, in the early 90s. Leslie had taken us on a driving tour of the city and pointed out the site of the World Trade Center as we'd driven past it. I had also traveled there on business a couple of times before, and I had always been intimidated by the city's immensity, crowdedness, and fast pace. I always felt like I was being hustled. Taxi drivers would complain if they didn't like the tip. Everything was so expensive. There was the constant sound of drivers honking and yelling at each other.

I felt just the opposite as we walked around Manhattan that Saturday afternoon. All the noise and hurry were gone. It was serene. We didn't have to walk in a frenzied pace on the sidewalks to avoid getting plowed over. We were able to cross the streets without dodging cars threatening to run us over. I remember thinking, *Wow, this city has been humbled by 9/11.*

We were walking around Times Square in the early part of Saturday afternoon when one of our twins said, "Hey, there's the WWF." It was a WWF-themed restaurant/nightclub—nothing fancy—but we remembered that Katie had worked there part-time as a waitress to help make ends meet. It was perfect timing: we were hungry. We decided to go in.

It wasn't busy at that time of day. It felt like we were the only customers. I led our group to a back section of the restaurant, ignoring other available sections and tables in the front. I didn't make a conscious decision to do that; it was as if a magnetic force took me to the rear section of the restaurant.

When we were seated, Phyllis introduced us and asked the wait-ress if she'd known Katie McCloskey. Stunned, the waitress, who was named Michelle, took a step backwards. She looked at us for a moment and didn't say a word. Then tears welled up in her eyes as she began to cry. Then we all started to cry. We hadn't yet spoken a word. She told us that Katie had been a very good friend of hers—and in fact, we were sitting in Katie's section! She then brought over the WWF manager, who'd also known Katie. We all started to cry all over again. Michelle and the manager shared stories about Katie, and expressed how they loved and missed her so much.

As we finished our meal, the manager returned to our table to tell us that the meal was on him, and that we were welcome to come back any time. We all felt that this wasn't just a coincidence. Angel Katie had led us to that place, to feel her presence through our interaction with her co-workers. It was a powerful moment.

We walked through a tunnel to get to the train back to our hotel. We came across a wall filled with messages: *Our thoughts and prayers are with you. God Bless America. We are praying for you.* The writing was in all forms: in large print, scribbled, drawn, in pen or magic marker. Most of it was in red, white, and blue. People expressed their condolences; survivors reached out to those they'd lost, telling them how much they were missed. I felt that these messages were an expression of individual grief, as well as of a community of survivors, and a way for those survivors to join others in saying goodbye. I heard their voices and felt their pain—but it was heartwarming.

On Sunday morning we headed for Ground Zero. We were anxious; we had no idea how to get there. We carried special passes for the "family viewing area" that Dick had mailed to us in advance, but our cab driver didn't know where this special viewing area was located. He stopped close to Ground Zero and directed us to ask a police officer who happened to be standing nearby. We walked over to the officer, then realized Angel Katie was with us once again when the officer said, "You enter the family viewing area right here."

Phyllis took the lead as we walked toward the area. She walked in earnest, with intensity and purpose. A few police officers silently greeted us, and Phyllis showed them our family pass. They nodded respectfully. It felt as if we were being solemnly greeted on our way into a funeral home. We ascended a few steps to a platform overlooking Ground Zero.

The sun was shining. A big American flag was waving in the cool breeze. It was cold, but comfortable—and very quiet. All you could hear was the noise of the flag clanging against the metal flagpole.

The platform was very small in contrast to the view. It felt as if we were standing on the edge of a cliff overlooking the Grand Canyon. There were just a few other people on the platform. Everyone whispered as if they were in a church.

As I gazed out onto Ground Zero, I was struck by how big it was—an immense, expansive crater. It was like entering a professional baseball or football stadium at a high level, and looking down onto the field—but in this instance it just was not one field, but several fields.

Earth-moving equipment, construction vehicles, tall cranes, and trucks blanketed the dirt- and snow-sprinkled surface. The land where the World Trade Center had once stood had turned into a hollow construction site.

It had been a little over five months since the North and South Towers had collapsed and burned to the ground. Yet the scars of a warzone, like you see in a war film or documentary, remained. Several of the surrounding buildings were scorched black from the heat and flames. Windows were missing or shattered. One tall building had a huge American flag draped across it.

We lingered for a while, mostly remaining in a silent meditative state. I said a prayer for Katie and for all of those who had perished that day. As we began to walk down the steps from the platform to the sidewalk, we turned to each other and acknowledged that we had just visited Katie's final resting place. It was sacred ground.

———

PART 2

We also rejoice in our sufferings, because we know that suffering produces perseverance; perseverance, character; and character, hope. And hope does not disappoint us, because God has poured out his love into our hearts by the Holy Spirit, whom he has given us.

—ROMANS 5: 3-5

CHAPTER SIX
Forging Ahead

Life went on, as it does.

Kristen and Katie returned to Westminster College to continue their first semester at college. Katie, like Kristen, turned to writing to deal with her grief. Mark immersed himself in his passion, music. He was selected to play percussion on the drum line of the high-school marching band, and participated with our church's hand bell ringers.

Phyllis continued to provide companion services to the elderly people in our community and attained a black belt in karate. She told me it helped her break the wood with her chops and swift kicks when she pretended the wood was Osama Bin Laden.

The McCloskey family established the Katie McCloskey Memorial Scholarship Fund with the Community Foundation of St. Joseph County, a local community foundation near South Bend.

I sought refuge in my work.

Less than a month after 9/11, my daughter Katie and I attended a Steelers game. It was a sunny but colder-than-normal fall afternoon at Heinz Field in Pittsburgh. At the end of the first half, the game festivities were suddenly interrupted. President George W. Bush appeared on the Jumbotron to announce that United States military forces had begun bombing Afghanistan in retaliation for the 9/11 terrorist attacks. The crowd of sixty thousand people in the football stadium became subdued. There was a prolonged period of impromptu silence. The clouds set in, and the weather seemed to become much colder. I put my arm around Katie and pulled her closer to me. My heart sank, because I knew where our country was headed.

I had a flashback to the documentaries of the Vietnam war, when the United States military took a scorched-earth approach and dropped 388,000 tons of napalm—an incendiary mixture of a gelling agent and a volatile petrochemical—on Vietnam, which erupted in huge fireballs. The burning gel stuck to the skin, causing widespread suffering, death, and destruction.

In the 1960s, I had watched the evening news coverage of the Vietnam war when the Secretary of Defense, Robert McNamara, a statistician by training, provided body-count statistics—how many Viet Cong the U.S. had killed—as a measure of success. I felt perplexed. *Are we taking a similar course of action in Afghanistan … kill all the Taliban to win the war on terror?*

Similar questions weighed heavy on my mind in the wake of Bush's announcement. *Why does our government always default to military action? Why do we justify this indiscriminate killing as the means to resolve problems? Don't we know by now that these incursions turn into decade-long debacles? Don't we know by now that we are feeding into a vicious cycle … that we reap what we sow? Won't our violent military action spawn a whole new generation of violent extremists who will grow up and be taught to hate America?*

The lyrics of Marvin Gaye's song, "What's Going On" rang in my head:

> *Mother, mother*
> *There's too many of you crying*
> *Brother, brother, brother*
> *There's far too many of you dying*
> *You know we've got to find a way to bring some lovin' here today*

Father, father
We don't need to escalate
You see, war is not the answer
For only love can conquer hate

In the days, weeks, and months following the bombing and invasion of Afghanistan, I began to think, with Gaye: *There must be a better way.*

———

From that time on, I started down a different path: to learn more about why the men had hijacked those planes on 9/11 to cause so much destruction, death, and suffering, and what had led them to resort to such violent action. I felt compelled to find the answers; I wanted to determine the root cause.

Angel Katie regularly appeared to me, almost every day—at least once a day, and sometimes twice a day, when I saw 9:11 in so many random places: on my desktop computer, cell phone, television, kitchen stove, microwave oven, and even at PNC Park during Pittsburgh Pirates games. Her 9:11 appearances reinforced my belief that she would guide me on this quest, and that I was not all alone on this journey. I just had to stick with it, no matter how long or how difficult it turned out to be.

I wondered: What could I do to contribute to a more peaceful world in the future?

In what I considered another very meaningful coincidence, I received a brochure shortly thereafter about a workshop on nonviolent communication from the Omega Institute in Rhinebeck, New York. The workshop emphasized the importance of compassion in human relationships and how to stop violence—both verbal and physical—in the world. I was already familiar with Omega, and I knew it would be a quality workshop.

I'd first attended a workshop at Omega back in 1992, and continued to attend workshops there afterward. Phyllis and I once took a couples massage workshop together there, and we love the place. It's in a rustic setting, nestled in the Hudson Valley about ninety miles north of New York City. Soon after you drive over the Hudson River, driving east from Pennsylvania, you encounter winding country roads and beautiful country, with rolling green pastures and plentiful horse farms. The village of Rhinebeck is an historic, quaint place. (One of our favorite restaurants is Beekman Arms Tavern, an historic landmark built in 1766; legend has it that George Washington dined there.) Omega's campus is a relatively short drive from the village, set back in the woods. And it's quiet: all you hear there are the sounds of nature.

I've always been comfortable at Omega. It's always a good place for me to get away, relax, meditate, eat healthily, contemplate, and search for direction and meaning. A few times before, during stressful times in my life or when I was on the cusp of a big life or career change, I had gone to Omega.

Now, I knew it was time to go again.

Marshall Rosenberg led the workshop. Marshall, who has since passed away, was an American psychologist who wrote many books on resolving conflict between people, in relationships, and in society. He also founded the Center for Nonviolent Communication (CNVC).

The workshop started on a Friday evening, as do most at Omega. Usually after a brief orientation, the workshop begins. But we received word that Marshall's flight had been delayed and he would be late, and so we listened to calm, soothing music in the interim. When Marshall arrived, he immediately got started. He had a presence about him like a seasoned professor: casual, conservatively dressed. He took a seat at the front of the classroom and began to talk with the participants. It was the opposite of a lecture, and very interactive. I was really surprised by how open the participants were; it was like a giant psychotherapy session. Marshall kept my interest and attention. I could tell he was an experienced teacher with a lot of wisdom. The time flew by that evening, and the workshop went into overtime.

The bulk of Saturday was spent in intense role-playing. A steady stream of participants role-played with Marshall, and he became a surrogate for the other person in one broken or abusive relationship after another. He illustrated, through his actions, the significance of listening, leading to empathy. Many participants became emotional, displayed anger, screamed at Marshall, broke down and cried. In many instances, it seemed apparent that this was the first time they'd had a voice—the first time any one had ever listened to them. My main takeaway from the workshop was the realization that we, as human beings, can develop nonviolent relationships by listening to one another, developing empathy, and building trust and respect.

———

The following year I would attend another Omega workshop titled "Claiming your place at the fire: Living the second half of your life on purpose." Led by Richard Leider—who'd written a book of the same title—this workshop, for me, was about finding your passion, leaving a legacy. It would prove another important step in my journey.

In December 2006, a little over five years after 9/11, Phyllis and I attended a graduation ceremony at LaRoche College, a small liberal arts college in Pittsburgh with a global perspective. Danit Fridman, the daughter of our friends Michael and Fortuna French, was graduating that evening. The keynote speaker, an alumnus of the Fletcher School—a Tufts University graduate school—spoke about global issues, focusing on global peace. This sparked my interest immensely.

When I got home that evening, I checked out the Fletcher School's website. I already knew that the Fletcher School was a world-renowned graduate school of international relations. I had applied there thirty years earlier as I was completing my undergraduate degree in Political Science at Duquesne University, but had not been accepted.

Now, sitting there reading about the Fletcher School again, I was struck by a sense of destiny—an urging that I had to attend that institution to develop a global perspective and find my vision.

The next morning, as Phyllis and I were having breakfast, I shared my experience from the night before with her. She reacted with a puzzled look. To my surprise, she told me the idea of me going to graduate school was ridiculous, and questioned why I was even giving this a thought.

My reply was anything but articulate as I struggled to describe what had happened the night before. I sheepishly sank back in my chair as she dismissively got up from the table and left the room.

———

What is going on here?

Am I crazy?

Isn't there an easier way?

I couldn't get these questions out of my head. But neither could I resist the powerful force I felt compelling me to attend the Fletcher School.

The clergy often refer to this kind of experience as answering one's calling. Others call it an epiphany. I describe it as an *opening*, because it was then that I became *open to the possibility* of the existence of the miraculous, a powerful force often referred to as grace—a force that was pushing me to transcend my normal life and instead live an extraordinary life, rooted in love.

Still, there was a $62,500 tuition bill standing in the way.

Yes, a year at the Fletcher School would cost nearly sixty-three thousand dollars—money we definitely did not have. And that wasn't even counting travel for the residency parts and other expenses. Fear set in, and I started to make a list of all the reasons I couldn't do this.

We already have a mortgage.

We're already paying off college student loans for Kristen and Katie.

We're already taking on additional debt to finance Mark's college education.

What was I thinking, even contemplating embarking on such an enormous undertaking at such enormous expense? Was I going through a midlife crisis? Should I even be considering something like this at my stage of life? Wasn't this biting off far more than I could chew?

Even considering this life-interrupting, expensive change at this point in my life pulled me back to a painful part of my childhood, when my father had lost his business and the family had abruptly become poor—and the trauma I had suffered from it.

———

CHAPTER SEVEN
Looking Back

The first part of my childhood had been idyllic, although of course I didn't realize it at the time. And that made the change—the point when things went very wrong for my family, financially and otherwise—harder to handle.

My parents, Elmer "Etz" and Rita Etzel, were good souls—honest, moral, and ethical. My mother often kiddingly accused my dad of being too honest, especially when it came to business matters. But when she herself had once found a hundred-dollar bill on the floor of an Atlantic City casino, she'd picked it up, held it high in the air and shouted out, "Did anyone lose this?"

When I look back as an adult, I realize that they were a bit innocent and naïve about the world around them. They'd both grown up in Brentwood—a suburb of Pittsburgh—as part of what Tom Brokaw referred to in his book as *The Greatest Generation*. They'd lived through the Great Depression and World War II, and my dad had enlisted in the Marines and seen the horrors of war close-up as he and his fellow marines stormed the beaches of the Pacific Islands held by the Japanese.

Their families came through the Great Depression pretty much unscathed, at least economically, but the memories of neighbors not having enough food and clothing always stayed with them. They counted themselves very fortunate.

Brentwood was a safe community with a spacious park and swimming pool, both within close walking distance from their homes. They did not have a care in the world while growing up. Although they ran in the same social circles, they did not date. Their romance started in "love letters" they wrote to each other while my dad was stationed in the Pacific during World War II. Those letters led to marriage soon after my father returned home after the end of the war.

They moved to Elderwood Drive, in Bethel Park, Pennsylvania, shortly after my brother was born. It was not long before they added three more children to the household: my older sister, myself, and then my younger sister.

My early childhood years growing up on Elderwood Drive were a lot like my parents' experience growing up in Brentwood: sheltered and simple. Then we moved to a brand-new house on Cassidy Drive, also in Bethel Park, in February of 1964, just around the time the Beatles made their debut in America and appeared on *The Ed Sullivan Show*. Many of the homes in the area were new. The houses on our street were either just constructed and up for sale by the contractor, or still under construction. The smell of freshly cut lumber permeated the neighborhood, and a steady pounding of hammers echoed in the background.

Our new house smelled fresh and new, like a brand-new automobile as you drive it off the car dealer's lot for the first time. My feet would sink into the plush wall-to-wall carpeting; the freshly painted walls were bright and cheery. The cozy living room, with a big fireplace, was surrounded by brand-new Colonial American style furniture. The dining room had a new table, China cabinet and hutch, all in Colonial American style. My three siblings and I each had our own bedroom, and the house included what were very modern amenities for the time: a laundry chute, a soft-water tank, a garbage disposal, an incinerator.

Though I was only nine years old, I could sense that my family was doing well. I felt secure. But my parents certainly did not have airs about them. In later years, they loved to tell the story of when they'd stopped by a car dealership to buy my mother a new car, a Chevrolet Corvair. They'd stood alone in the showroom, and the salesmen had totally ignored them. My parents soon realized that it was because of how they were dressed. Eventually a salesman had reluctantly wandered over to them, and my parents always laughed about the astonished look that had appeared on the salesman's face when my dad had pulled out a wad of cash from his pocket to pay for the car.

From 1960 to 1967, my dad owned and operated a teenage dance hall, the Lebanon Lodge. Teenage dances were a big deal in the 1960s. They were where the teenagers of the Baby Boomer generation congregated, the meeting places for teenage boys and girls. The music was a big part of it, no doubt; the best DJs had unique record collections and followings. The "real" popular dance music was not played on the radio stations—back then, there were only AM stations. A good DJ knew how to start the music out slow, gradually build the crowd into a frenzy, and then bring the crowd under control with a slow dance set, before starting the cycle all over again.

My dad always talked at the dinner table about how the crowd was the key to the business. The music was important; the atmosphere played a big part too. But without a big crowd, you had nothing. My dad was proud to say that he started with a crowd of twelve teenagers in 1960, and at its peak, the Lodge packed the place with a thousand foot-stomping, hand-clapping, screaming and yelling teenagers every Friday and Saturday night.

To unwind after those stressful Friday and Saturday night dances, my dad enjoyed taking Sunday drives to a mountain resort under development near Cumberland, Maryland. I remember his right wrist dangling over the steering wheel of our big Pontiac Bonneville as we cruised into the mountains. (My mother disliked the car, which she referred to as a boat.) I remember sitting with my parents at a picnic table in the woods, surrounded by big granite boulders, as they signed papers and purchased a plot of land with the intent to build a cabin on the man-made lake, still under development. And my dad was actively looking into purchasing a Roy Rogers restaurant franchise at the time as well.

Then, suddenly, the bottom fell out. My dad would later say that the rug was pulled out from under us.

———

What happened was simply the effect of a sweeping cultural change. In the "Summer of Love" in 1967, hippies and flower children came to prominence in San Francisco, and soon after spread to the rest of the country. The old music was out, and bands like the Grateful Dead and Jefferson Airplane were in. Young people began to leave the dance halls and migrate to coffee houses.

This was the beginning of the end of the Lebanon Lodge.

It took less than a year. The crowds at the Lodge became smaller and smaller, then finally disappeared. As my dad had said, the crowd was the magic—and within months, that magic evaporated.

I never understood the pressure my father must have been under until I became a parent myself and took on the responsibilities of raising my own family. He was watching his business, his income, disappear rapidly, and he had no plan B. He didn't know what to do, and he ended up giving up the business to a competitor. No money exchanged hands; my dad just wanted out. It was too much pressure for him. My dad simply didn't believe that he had the staying power to ride it out and take the time to seek alternatives, to adapt. So he got out.

He never recovered from the loss of that business, the end of that eight-year run of success. He looked for a job, but after running his own business, he found it impossible to go back and work for anyone else. He didn't want to be a flunky—and he believed that he didn't have the education or the skill set to find a meaningful job. Ultimately, he did nothing.

The wheels started to come off at home, too. My folks sold the house on Cassidy Drive in a down market, and we moved to a rental home on Brightwood Road, in another part of Bethel Park. Nothing in their lives up to then had prepared my parents for this.

———

I turned fourteen years old during the time my family lived on Brightwood Road. It was the worst year of my life while growing up—the time I first felt despair.

The house on Brightwood was very small; the furniture from Cassidy Drive didn't fit in it. The furniture had been purchased new, customized for a much bigger house, but the house on Brightwood was cramped. I could hardly walk in my bedroom, let alone open the drawers of my bedroom hutch.

The house was dark. The windows didn't admit much sunshine. It was if there was a dark cloud hovering over the house, always. To match this darkness, the house had a musty, mildewy smell, like an old, rustic cottage on a lake—the opposite of the fresh, new, clean smell of the house on Cassidy Drive.

I saw my dad sink into a deep, debilitating depression. He spent most of that first year lying on the couch in our dark living room. He talked to himself, repeating the words, "Should have stayed on Elderwood, should have stayed on Elderwood." He rarely bathed or changed his clothes.

I didn't know what was going on; nothing made sense. I just knew that something was horribly wrong with my dad. I felt helpless, I felt ashamed, but I couldn't help him. My mother tried to motivate him by yelling and screaming. This just upset me more. The whole situation broke my heart.

During that time I saw, first-hand, how certain human conditions can make people ripe for violence: hopelessness, powerlessness, isolation, loneliness, no voice, no one listening, an absence of empathy. All of this could turn someone toward violent action. I knew my father was not a violent man. But one winter Sunday morning, I saw a side of him I had never seen before, as piece by piece, he picked up all the furniture in the living room and threw it all over the room. Chairs, couch, and end tables flew all about and crashed loudly into the living-room walls. The house shook as if we were in the middle of an earthquake. It was utter chaos.

I stood in complete shock at the entrance to the living room. I don't remember what had sparked my father's rage, if anything had. Perhaps his immense frustration had just hit a boiling point and erupted. But it really scared me. I was afraid he would physically harm me, my younger sister, my mother. I looked at my mother, standing next to me. She, too, was very frightened. It was the first time in my life that I saw real fear in her eyes: they were wide open in a brief, frozen gaze.

With hardly a moment of hesitation, my mom whisked me and my sister away, out the front door, and we made a quick dash to our car parked in the driveway. We didn't even grab our winter coats on our way out the front door.

We drove to my aunt's house and stayed there for the day. My mom telephoned Phil, a family friend who was a psychologist, and asked him to go over to the house and check on my dad. Phil spent the better part of that Sunday with my dad. After dinner, we returned to the house after getting assurance from Phil that it was safe.

When we returned home and walked through the front door, we stopped at the living-room entrance. I didn't know what to expect. But my dad was sitting on the couch, and all the furniture was put back into place. My dad's fury had been subdued.

My mom asked, "How are you doing?"

He replied, apologetically, "I couldn't keep it in anymore." He said he was glad that Phil had come over, that he had needed someone to talk to. My mom consoled him. This was just one of many instances when my mother rose to the occasion, while working hard to hold our family together.

As an adult, I now realize that this experience was an inflection point in my life. Simply put, my dad felt that he didn't have a voice. His frustration had been walled up until he couldn't take it anymore, and he'd exploded into violent action. The event led me to place value in dialogue, to find my voice, and to seek help from others from that point forward, in various conscious and unconscious ways. Unwittingly, I was drawn to Marshall Rosenberg's nonviolent communication workshop because of this experience, rooted deeply in my soul. And that workshop, in turn, led me on a path to expand my voice even further and reach others on a global stage.

Other events would have similarly far-reaching effects on my life. In another incident later that same winter, I saw how suddenly disrespect could incite violence. My brother disparaged my father, yelling, "You're a terrible father, you're a bum." I think this was the final straw for my dad. He jumped up from the couch, took a few quick steps towards my brother and started to swing a punch. I was standing nearby, and my body reacted without my thinking—I lunged between the two of them with my arms outstretched. In essence, I instinctively broke up a fight just before it started. This was my first action as a peace builder. It was an awful, ugly moment, and the emotional damage was significant; I cried that night in bed. It would forever leave a mark on my psyche. But that too would prove lastingly meaningful to me, down the line. Violent words and actions and disrespect became abhorrent to me from that point forward—and it led me to seek nonviolent conflict resolution for the rest of my life.

By April of 1969 my mom realized that we all needed to get out of that rental house on Brightwood Road. It's fair to say that the whole family was depressed, and it was tearing us apart. Luckily, my mother inherited some money from the settlement of her mother's estate, and she was able to put a substantial down payment on a house located on Highland Road in Bethel Park. It was the fourth house we would live in during that five-year span.

But we still had very little money, so we had to get food stamps. It was embarrassing to have to use the stamps at the checkout line at the grocery store. It seemed that everyone in the line was staring at you when you handed over the stamps to pay for your groceries, and I felt shame every time. This life experience became a source of empathy for me later in life, when I witnessed others struggling in a similar plight.

When I went to high school at Bethel Park High School, I was eligible for free lunches. I had to go to the principal's office every morning to pick up my ticket for that day's lunch. That too, was embarrassing. But the secretary was very nice, and non-judgmental. I was grateful to get the lunch ticket, and I knew it eased my mother's financial burden.

But we struggled with other financial stresses. Several times, my mom had to take a taxi to work because the car had broken down—my family simply didn't have enough money to get it fixed. And there seemed to be an endless worry that the utilities companies would shut off the electricity and gas because we couldn't pay the bills.

One memory really stands out in my mind from this time. My dad, my mom, and I were driving home one cold and dark winter evening, and as we approached a McDonald's I asked if we could stop and get a hamburger. My parents reacted to my request with anger and frustration: "How dare you ask to stop for a hamburger at McDonald's! You just don't get it, do you, Tommy? We don't have any money!" When all of this went down, I didn't say another word, but I saw my dad in the rear-view mirror, looking at me with tears streaming down his cheek. *Things are so bad that we can't even buy a hamburger?* I thought. This left an indelible memory.

That same evening, my parents started to talk about getting a divorce, right in front of me. I broke down, crying and pleading with them to stay together. I told them a divorce wouldn't make things any better … I wanted our family to stay together, no matter what.

In the end, they listened to me. They stayed together.

———

I found refuge on the basketball court. I was lucky enough to play for the Bethel Park High School basketball team, and during the season, after we finished practice and showered, it was usually around 6:00 p.m., and I headed home via a long walk. It was wintertime, and dark by the time I left the gymnasium. There was a shortcut through the woods at the far end of the school campus, which led to Bethel Church Road, a main road in the direction of my house on Highland Road.

The walk through the dark woods was a time of solitude, a moment of respite for me. It was quiet and peaceful. The light from the moon would shine through the trees, providing enough visibility for me to find my way on the snow-covered path. Occasionally I heard the crackling noise of an animal scampering off into the night. Initially that noise would startle me, but I grew accustomed to it. As I walked, all bundled up in my winter cap, gloves, and scarf and lugging my books and gym bag, I would reflect on the day in school, and that night's practice. As I got close to the end of the path out of the woods, I would begin to see the headlights and hear the slushy sound of tires speeding along on the snowy, sometimes icy Bethel Church Road. I always knew that this was the end of my brief respite, and my mind would shift to worry—anxiety about what was happening at home. All I hoped for was that I could have some peace and quiet while I ate dinner (my mother always had a hot meal ready for me in the oven and a secret stash of chocolate bars in the cabinet) and get to my homework before I hit the mattress, pretty much exhausted from a full day of school and basketball.

Those adolescent years had quite an impact on me. I became very serious, very driven. I grew up fast, what seemed like overnight—I believed that I had to rely on myself. In the summertime I worked as a caddy at a local country club, and the dew, glistening on the green fairways in the bright sunshine, was a welcome sight on those summer mornings. The sun, fresh air, and vast open space gave me a sense of being free and easy. It provided me with some much-needed solace.

———

CHAPTER EIGHT
Sunshine Emerges

I n the summer of 1972, the summer before my senior year at Bethel Park High School, I saw a glimmer of hope at home.

My dad was ready to give it another try in the dance business. And my mother, God bless her soul, not only stood by his side, but selflessly partnered with him again. Winston Churchill was famous for saying, "Success is not final, failure is not fatal: it is the courage to continue that counts." This quote was fitting for my mom and dad.

The summer started off with four straight weeks of rainfall. The water levels of Pittsburgh's three rivers (the Allegheny, Monongahela, and Ohio), already high, were exacerbated by the effects of Hurricane Agnes on June 24, 1972, which turned out to be the worst flooding event in the city since 1942.

Normally, I would be caddying every day at the country club in the month of June. But that soggy month of 1972, I helped my dad paint the inside of the building that would soon become his new club, The Image.

The rain ended and the sunshine returned to Pittsburgh. For me, it felt like the dawn of a new era. The Image opened on Sunday night, July 16, 1972—coincidentally my mom and dad's twenty-fifth wedding anniversary.

My mom and dad, my older sister, and I rode down to The Image together that evening. My sister was three years older than me and lived at home; after graduating from high school, she had gone to work at a bank in downtown Pittsburgh. She hung in there during the tough times in our family and remained steadfast in support of my parents. It felt like we were working together as a family again. That was a sensation I hadn't experienced since we lived on Cassidy Drive, and I relished it. We were climbing out of the abyss.

My job was to stand close to the edge of the property and direct traffic to the parking lot across the street. I was pleasantly amazed as I watched the steady, seemingly endless stream of cars drive down the hill from Route 88 and flow into the parking lot, as if it were a well-established routine.

That evening, our venue drew an overwhelming near-capacity crowd of over five hundred. As they traversed the parking lot across the street, a vibrant parade of eager attendees formed, snaking their way into a lengthy queue that stretched outside the entrance of The Image. The resonant echoes of rock-and-roll music reverberated through the air, its thumping bass guitar causing the very walls of the building to tremble. The atmosphere crackled with palpable anticipation; you could practically taste the electric buzz of the crowd's excitement.

Overwhelmed by sheer joy, I could not contain my elation at the sight of such a multitude of people. It felt like a page torn straight out of the Woodstock era—already iconic, though a mere three years had passed since. The scene unfolded before me, painting a vivid portrait of a peace-loving and affable community of hippies. Many sported cascading locks of hair that flowed freely, their attire consisting of tie-dyed shirts, loose-fitting garments, or ethereal halter tops. Bell-bottom pants and frayed jeans danced alongside ankle-length dresses, creating a swirling symphony of countercultural fashion. Among the crowd, a handful of girls adorned their faces with the whimsical charm of funky-looking granny glasses, adding an extra touch of bohemian allure to the gathering.

Early in the evening, the driver of a pick-up truck defied my directions, drove past me, and proceeded to park in the very small parking area adjacent to The Image. A young hippie girl, sitting in the front seat, jumped up and practically climbed out of her seat, noticeably staring at me as they drove past.

As night fell and the outside world settled into a serene stillness, my attention was captivated by the arrival of the free-spirited hippie girl. She gracefully departed the building and sauntered towards me, while I stood beneath the radiant glow of a floodlight, fulfilling my duty. It became unmistakably clear that her purposeful strides were aimed at me, as she sought to greet me and introduce herself. With admiration in her eyes, she complimented my voluminous Afro. An aura of serenity emanated from her, and her physical allure was undeniable—her flowing reddish-brown hair danced in contrast to her piercing, deep-blue eyes. Amid our conversation, my father nonchalantly passed by, causing me to blush with embarrassment. Realizing that engaging too long with the hippie girl was inappropriate, given my duty-bound position, I hastily explained that my father, the owner of The Image, had just walked past. She got the message and hastily retreated toward the building. I never saw her again.

I was determined to ensure The Image's successful launch, and my commitment to assisting my dad that night remained resolute. Not even the enchantment of the hippie girl could sway me from my purpose.

CHAPTER NINE

Love at First Sight

Just a few months later, on October 21, 1972, my life changed abruptly, and forever.

It started out as a normal Saturday night at The Image. The band Timothy performed before a crowd of approximately four hundred high-school teenagers. I hung out in the DJ booth perched above the dance floor, a faint light shining on my Afro hairdo. As the club DJ, I would play records during the band's breaks. Many tools were at my disposal: a state-of-the art sound system, an intricate dance of lights that synchronized with the music, pulsating in mesmerizing hues; a hypnotic strobe light that wove an enchanting slow-motion illusion as people swayed and swirled; and to top it all, my personal favorite: a mystical crystal ball gracefully revolving above the dance floor, reflecting beams of light that cast a spellbinding glow upon the revelers below.

At the end of my last session of the evening, I was summoned by one of the security folks. He told me that a high-school friend of mine, Clifford, wanted to speak with me. So I went down to the balcony and Clifford was waiting for me at the foot of the stairs of the balcony. He told me that a girl from Fontbonne Academy, an all-girl Catholic high school, wanted to meet me. He pointed toward where she stood at the edge of the dance floor with a couple of other girls. He and I walked over to her, and he introduced us.

That was when I met Phyllis McCloskey.

Her physical beauty struck me instantly, leaving me momentarily breathless. Her eyes, shining with warmth and kindness, beckoned me into a world of unspoken connection. Her figure, shaped with a captivating allure, drew my gaze irresistibly. Every curve seemed to be a work of art. And there was a genuine essence that radiated from within. A tender and authentic spirit seemed to pour forth whenever her lips curved into a smile, which happened frequently.

I asked Phyllis if she wanted to dance, and she said okay. She was the first girl I'd ever asked to dance with me—even though I was the DJ, I was quite shy about dancing. I compared myself to many of the outstanding dancers I watched below me on the dance floor, and I didn't think that I was very good.

Before we knew it, the midnight hour was closing in on us. Phyllis was driving and had to be home by midnight, so I offered to walk her to her car in the parking lot across the street. She said okay, and went to get her two friends as I headed out the front entrance.

As she emerged from the building, bathed in the radiant glow of the floodlights that illuminated the entrance, I was captivated by her enchanting beauty, which surpassed even the charm she'd exuded inside the softly lit dance hall. Like a silky waterfall, her luscious chestnut-brown hair cascaded down to her hips, creating an aura of elegance and allure. Her rich, warm brown eyes sparkled and danced like precious gems as they caught the glimmers of the lights. Within their depths, I could glimpse a world of mystery and emotion, drawing me in like a mesmerizing whirlpool.

She introduced me to her two friends from Fontbonne Academy, Mary Malia and Kathleen Rooney. Mary was talkative, outgoing, and bubbly; Kathleen seemed quiet and shy, looking down at the ground after she said hello.

As we reached her car, Phyllis and I indulged in a tender embrace, our lips interlocking in a sublime moment that seemed to transcend time itself, as if we were two souls who had traversed lifetimes together and finally reunited in this fleeting instance. I told her I hoped she would return to The Image the following Saturday evening.

As I reluctantly began to walk away from the car, I really hoped I would see her again. Deep within my soul, I intuited an unspoken bond that connected us beyond the realm of mere chance encounters. There was an intangible quality that set Phyllis apart—a luminous aura brimming with inherent goodness and unwavering strength, drawing me inexorably toward her like a celestial force guiding two destined souls together.

Upon reentering the building, I found my mother settled within her cashier booth, positioned at the entrance. A knowing smile played on her lips as she observed my uncharacteristic act of escorting a girl to the parking lot—a departure from my usual post-dance routine. "Who was that babe?" she asked. Amusement danced in my eyes as I shared her hearty laugh, leaving her question unanswered and allowing a sense of mystery to linger in the air. Unbeknownst to her, that very babe would ultimately become a beloved daughter-in-law, bridging our lives in an unbreakable bond within a span of fewer than five years.

Phyllis returned to The Image the following Saturday night. She and I spent the entire evening talking as we sat at a table on the balcony. Our only interruptions came when I had to occasionally scurry back to the DJ booth to play records while the band took their break. Our conversation was substantial. She told me her father was a physician, a gynecologist in Mt. Lebanon, and that her mother had died from alcoholism when Phyllis was only twelve years old. She talked a lot about Isy (short for Isabel), who I later realized was an angel in Phyllis's life. Isy had come to the McCloskey family to help Phyllis's mother after she'd come home from the hospital after Phyllis's birth. She was supposed to stay for two weeks, but two weeks turned into eighteen years as Isy became Phyllis's surrogate mother. When Phyllis's mother's health deteriorated from her alcoholism, Isy stepped up and provided Phyllis with unconditional love and nurturing. When Phyllis's mother was near death, Isy promised her that she would finish raising Phyllis until she went to college.

The way Phyllis talked about Isy left an indelible impression on me; it was evident how much she loved her. This was a prelude to my lifetime of witnessing Phyllis's huge capacity to love.

A glimpse of Phyllis's competitive nature came through that evening too, when I told her about my love of playing basketball and how I'd chosen not to play at Bethel Park High School my senior year in order to help my dad with The Image. She told me that she enjoyed playing basketball as well, and challenged me to a game of one-on-one. Little did I know at the time about the athletic prowess of Phyllis McCloskey!

Phyllis and I exchanged phone numbers at the end of the evening, and we started dating the following weekend.

———

After I met Phyllis, the shadow that had hovered over me for the previous five-year period was lifted. In fact, the shadow vanished. She changed my life forever. Years later, I realized that she'd saved my life. She had become my angel.

After I met her, things changed for the better. The gates of heaven were opened and I was overcome by a flood of bright sunshine. The atmosphere of toxic negativity that had dominated my life before Phyllis was eradicated, and she introduced me to a life full of contagious positivity. This was a whole new way of living for me. Life became vibrant, full of adventure and *fun*. I was all in.

Phyllis was all in as well. She wrote in her journal in early 1973, just a few months after we first met:

> Laid in bed last night and thanked God for letting October 21, 1972, happen to me. It was a door that was opened in my life that had a very beautiful world inside it.
>
> For a while, I stood at the doorway without entering for fear I might stumble and fall, and be stepped on once again—but as time went on, I grew less and less scared of what I saw and began to step slowly,
>
> One step led to the next. I sometimes hesitated not knowing what would happen next, but he held my hand and helped me to understand it all.
>
> Letting go of my hand, he left one day and then I was on my own.
>
> I could turn around and walk back out that door, knowing I would never ever return again, but I couldn't give this beautiful world up and so I waited …
>
> Until one day he took my hand again and we walked on …

CHAPTER TEN
Taking the Plunge

Now, though thirty-five years had passed since I had met Phyllis and escaped from that dark chapter in my life, all those negative thoughts and emotions re-emerged as I wondered how I was going to pay for the Fletcher School's $62,500 tuition bill. Money was the main obstacle. I also realized that this was a big change I was considering—there was so much unknown. I wondered whether it was all worth the risk, and I knew I didn't want to return to that dark place ever again. I found it hard to get beyond my past, to take that first step. Those bad memories kept creeping up, and fear stood in my way.

Still, throughout 2007, I found myself drawn to the Fletcher School's website. I reviewed the website repeatedly, each time making excuses in my mind as to why I shouldn't apply—primarily the expense and time commitment, which the website estimated at twenty hours per week. But underlying all that was the memory of our time on Brightwood Road, a memory that still haunted me. I couldn't get the images out of my mind of my dad on the couch, talking to himself. Was I going to go down a similar path and cause financial devastation to my family?

I felt there was no point in sharing this internal struggle about money matters with Phyllis. By this point in our life together, she had grown weary of my anxiety over money. But on January 1, 2008, I shared my New Year's resolution with her: I would make an inquiry with the Fletcher School about their graduate program. To my disappointment, she responded with irritation. That was it—no further discussion or disagreement about it.

Then, shortly after the holiday season, I found the courage to take the difficult first step of looking into the program. I felt a sense of relief from my anxiety about the unknown as I dialed the phone number of the Fletcher School Admissions Department. I was greeted by the friendly voice of a woman named Nicki Sass. I told her I wasn't sure if I was calling the right person, or the right department—I had found the contact information on the website a bit confusing–and she assured me that she was the right person.

I told her about my interest in the mid-career program, the Global Master of Arts Program (GMAP)—a one-year program that seemed ideally suited for working professionals. I told Nicki I was concerned about the potential time commitment and whether I could juggle my time between the studies and my CPA practice. Nicki encouraged me to at least come and visit the school. She told me that the class of 2008 would be on campus to take final exams in the middle of July, so I would be able to meet with them. She said she would arrange a meeting with the dean, Deborah Nutter, as well. We set the date on our calendars, and after hanging up, I said to myself, *Wow, now that wasn't so hard. And, really, what do I have to lose by just taking a trip to Boston?*

Before I made my travel arrangements, I told Phyllis that I intended to visit the Fletcher School in Boston in July. She challenged me to explain why I was doing this. When I replied that I just needed to explore this—that even I doubted that anything would materialize—she shrugged her shoulders, rolled her eyes, and scoffed.

In July, I flew to Boston a day before the meetings to ensure I'd make it on time. I arrived in the afternoon and checked into a bed-and-breakfast within a short walk of the Tufts University campus.

It was a sunny, hot, and humid summer afternoon in Boston, and I took a lengthy walk around the Tufts campus. Several older buildings were well preserved, which suggested to me that the university held a high regard for its history. I liked that there was a lot of open space with well-manicured green lawns. It was quiet; the students were away on summer break. I found the Cabot Building, with a big sign outside of the building that read *The Fletcher School of Law and Diplomacy, founded 1933*. I gazed at the sign for a few minutes, remembering that the Fletcher School was the oldest graduate school of international relations in the country.

By that time it was late afternoon, and I decided to head back to the bed-and-breakfast. I walked down from campus and came upon Davis Square. There was a lot of activity—an abundance of people of all ages, hanging out. There was a strong sense of community here. I was impressed that the city supported bicycle riders; there were many young people riding bicycles in the bicycle lanes on the busy streets. It was clearly more progressive than Pittsburgh—this was something that Pittsburgh did not have at the time.

Hunger began to set in, and I stopped for dinner at an Italian place. After dinner, on the way back to the B&B, I started to get that familiar butterfly feeling in my stomach, just like when I was a kid at the start of a competitive basketball or football game. I was feeling the kind of nervousness that means something big, important, and life-changing is happening.

In anticipation of the big day ahead of me, I had a restless night's sleep, tossing and turning only to wake at the crack of dawn. The B&B owner provided some juice, coffee, and pastries, but I was too nervous to eat anything—the butterflies were back. It felt like I was headed to a job interview for my dream job.

The receptionist greeted me warmly as I walked into the lobby of the Fletcher School. As the elevator landed, I heard the clang of the bell and the shuffling of the doors. Nicki Sass exited and approached me with a big smile, extending her hand. She had an air of genuineness about her—no superficial airs, no pretense. Her friendliness and warmth reminded me of my daughters, and I felt immediately at home.

When we got to Nicki's office—and after a brief discussion about the Boston Red Sox—she got down to business. Sitting in her chair behind her desk, she leaned forward and asked me the all-important question: "So, Tom, why do you want to attend the Fletcher School?"

I leaned forward towards her, tears welling up in my eyes. "A personal tragedy has brought me here," I said. "My niece and my high-school friend were killed on 9/11." Nicki's reaction gave me pause; it was different from anything I ever experienced. She was silent as she sank back in her chair, looked down at her desk, and sighed. She didn't look at me or say anything, but I felt that her empathy showed through her body language. That was more poignant than words.

"I know that the Fletcher School is a world-renowned school of international studies," I continued. "It's the best, in my opinion. I want to study here to find ways to reduce violent conflict in this world and head off another 9/11-type event from ever happening again."

Nicki, seeming a bit stunned, got up from her desk. "Let's take a tour of the campus," she said.

She took me on a quick tour, pointing out the dormitory where the GMAPers stayed while we walked past it. I had to laugh to myself—here I was, almost fifty-four years old and looking at my possible future dormitory. I was confident that I knew all about the Fletcher School. But Nicki shed some light on another important aspect of the school that I had overlooked: its strong sense of community. As we strolled along, we also discussed the application process, the school's history, and its reputation. I was wondering if I should mention my application and visit to the Fletcher School three decades before ... but it wasn't a happy memory, so I didn't bring it up.

We returned to the Cabot Building, and Nicki introduced me to Dean Nutter. We sat down in the dean's office—me on a couch, and her in a chair across from me. It seemed to me that her chair was elevated above me, as if she was looking down on me, and I felt uncomfortable as her eyes scanned me from the top of my head to the tips of my shoes. Had I dressed appropriately? Should I have worn a suit?

Dean Nutter asked me how I found the Fletcher School, and I shared my story about how I'd applied to the Fletcher School years before. She didn't ask any questions, and it appeared to me that her mind was somewhere else, distracted. Our meeting ended quickly—seemingly too quickly. Would this hurt me in the application process? I knew that the program catered to mid-career professionals with diplomatic and international organization work experience, and I had none.

After our meeting with Dean Nutter, Nicki took me to the Mugar Café to join the GMAP students for lunch. I sat down at a table with two students: a man who was a U.S. military officer, and an American man who worked for a non-governmental organization (NGO) in Africa. Soon other students began to straggle into the café, and several others joined us. They had just completed their International Law final exam. The quiet café was suddenly full of loud and cheerful conversation, and I sensed camaraderie among the boisterous group.

The students were from all around the world. They were friendly, welcoming, and eager to help me, and I appreciated their honesty. They didn't sugarcoat the reality of the program, but told me to expect an enormous amount of reading and writing. They described the GMAP team approach, in which the class was broken down into teams of five to six students. This helped you stay connected, especially when you returned home after the residency to study remotely. They mentioned that they used Skype to communicate. I had no idea what Skype was, but they enthusiastically told me several times that I could do it, and encouraged me to apply.

Nicki and I returned to her office to wrap up my visit. As she walked me to the elevator, we talked about the application process and deadline. I asked her about financial aid and potential scholarships. She told me that scholarships were minimal and usually earmarked for international students, to help them with their travel expenses.

As the elevator door opened, I turned to Nicki and asked, "So why is Fletcher so expensive?"

She replied, with her warm and friendly smile, "Because it's Fletcher."

———

Not long after this, I returned to the Omega Institute for Holistic Studies in Rhinebeck for a "wellness weekend"—no specific educational program, but rest, relaxation, meditation, massage therapy, and healthy organic food. My son Mark accompanied me on the trip.

When I arrived on Friday afternoon, I signed-up for a one-hour astrological consultation with Mwezi Mtoto, a humanistic astrologer. I signed Mark up for a one-hour massage therapy session in the same time slot. I'd had no intention to do this astrological consultation when I registered for the wellness weekend. It was, I felt, totally random. I was confident it was legitimate, because the session was offered through Omega's Wellness Center, but I had never done anything like this before—I admit, I'd always been a bit skeptical of this kind of stuff! But afterwards I realized that it had been Angel

Katie guiding me again.

The session took place in a tiny rustic building on the Omega campus, just a short walk along a wood-chip path down the hill from the dining hall. I'd walked past this structure many times over the years as I visited Omega. You would miss it if you weren't looking for it, and I had never noticed it until then. It was tiny inside—just enough room for two people to sit and talk.

As I walked into the building, I heard the vibrating of a window air conditioner. There wasn't a lot of natural sunlight in the room, but it wasn't dark either. Soft music played in the background.

Mwezi was seated behind a small desk. She was very large in stature. I think she told me she was born in Africa; she had a charming accent, and wore a dress full of bright colors. She was animated and shared her thundering laughter with me throughout the one-hour session. This didn't just come intermittently in bursts, but frequently, often mid-sentence. The walls seemed to shake from her laughter, it was so loud and contagious.

Mwezi went right to work the second I sat down across from her. I didn't know what to expect from an astrological consultation, but the session helped me understand myself and my evolution through my life by examining all the energies I'd been born with. Mwezi explained that this was known as the natal chart, and as she examined my natal chart she told me how the major transits—i.e., the planetary movements in the sky at that moment—would be affecting my chart for the next three years, 2008 through 2011.

I'm a Libra, and Mwezi told me quite a bit about what that meant for me. Libras have pleasant energy, and people are drawn to them. They have a flair for charm, mediation, and diplomacy, and they have strong feelings about being fair. Libra energy is intellectual, objective, balanced, serious. This all made sense to me.

She then pointed out something I'd never known: I had four planets in Scorpio in my natal chart at the time of my birth, which Mwezi said was very unusual. Scorpios have the most emotional energy—in fact, they possess intense energy, very deep emotions. She said that Scorpio's motto is *I desire.* "The Scorpio desire will run roughshod over Libra," she said. "Anything you want to do—you will do it. Anything you want to get—you will get it."

I said out loud, "Now this is starting to make sense." In my life up to that point, the Libra energy (intellectual, objective, balanced) had thwarted the Scorpio energy (intense emotion and desire). But there were a few times in my life when the typical Scorpio "tunnel vision" had kicked in. Mwezi pointed out that I needed to honor both sides—my Libra and my Scorpio energies—to stay healthy. She suggested that my emotional Scorpio side had been oppressed throughout most of my life.

My parents had often remarked on my tendency to get too emotional, which embarrassed and shamed me—so I had built a protective wall in those formative years. That wall was well in place as I reached adulthood, which drove Phyllis crazy because emotional intimacy was nearly impossible in our marriage. Through Phyllis's urging, I spent many years in psychotherapy to try to rectify that.

Mwezi told me that my walls were starting to show some cracks, and that my intense emotional energy was what drew people to me. She wanted me to learn an important life lesson: that it would not kill me to open up. "After all," she said, "your intense emotion is your strength. You are strong. You are resilient. You know how to recover. You are deep—you are ... very ... *heavy!*" And she let out one of her boisterous laughs.

I began to realize that this was more than an astrological consultation. Mwezi was an angel placed in my life. She told me to learn to trust myself—my intuition and insight, and my innate power of perception. She told me to "suspend my intellectual judgment, and to follow my intuition." She forecast that by doing this, I would be taken to an unpleasant place—but that I should allow it to happen, because it would lead me to a pleasant place afterward. "Just allow yourself to be led and guided," she said. "Everything will work out fine."

Her words blew me away. But she wasn't finished yet.

She told me I was a "wild man," in the sense that things that moved me were radical. Radical meant that I had to start something on my own, as an individual, to help others. Radical meant that simply writing a check to a charity was not going to be enough for me. Radical meant that I had to dig deeper, at the grassroots level, and be innovative. She was on target when she said that I had a desire to be an individual, and if I didn't speak up, it was "crazy-making, crippling, to try to contain your energy." She encouraged me not to conform, but to be creative, and insisted that I had a strong desire to help people. I had overcome much hardship in my life, she said, and now was the time to channel my empathy and energy into my altruistic desires.

"Your emotion is your power," she reemphasized. "Don't deny it—it's a gift. This is a period in your life when you are full of intuition and emotion, tuned-up, free from self-imposed restrictions. You are going through an awakening, and it is quite liberating."

Her written report would later summarize:

"Your career or contribution to the world at large is likely to touch many people's lives in a very positive, helpful way. You aim high and have an innate confidence and trust both in your own abilities and in life in general, which enables you to go far. You want to do something BIG with your life, and you attract the support you need to do so, for your aims are not solely for your own personal benefit. You want to give something back to the world, or to improve others' lives as well as your own."

That one-hour meeting with Mwezi was both a revelation and an affirmation. Again, what she called an awakening, I was calling an opening, and my heart told me she was spot-on; all I had to do was take off the brakes. I was on the right path.

As I said good-bye to Mwezi and left that little building on Omega's campus, I began to realize that all of my self-imposed restrictions were rooted in fear—fear of failure, fear of judgment, fear of the unknown. But as I gazed into the mirror of self-reflection, I saw the spark of potential that lay dormant within me, waiting to be unleashed. It was time to break free from the shackles of fear and embrace the limitless possibilities that lay ahead.

CHAPTER ELEVEN
The Leap of Faith

After my visit to the Fletcher School, Phyllis and I discussed the time requirement and the financial obligation that would be involved. She wasn't in favor of me even applying to the Fletcher School, but I told her that I wanted to consult with two good friends and trusted mentors, Bill Markus and the Reverend H. Pat Albright, before I reached a decision on whether to apply or not. Phyllis knew both Bill and Pat very well, but though I invited her to join me in these meetings, she declined.

We had known Pat for about five years. He was a retired Methodist minister who served as an associate pastor on our Presbyterian church's staff. In his late seventies, he was still actively engaged in ministry, and led our Bible study on Sunday mornings. His soft voice, passionate storytelling, and unique sense of humor drew a large following. He was old school, in our opinion—he was always available to meet, and he really listened. He often took the time to write us kind notes of encouragement, and wasn't hesitant to offer his honest opinion without sugar-coating anything. We valued his wisdom.

Soon after my visits to the Fletcher School and Omega Institute, Pat and I met for breakfast at my favorite breakfast place, the Village Dairy, in the Lebanon Shops just down the street from my home. He and I sat in a booth near the entrance. The smell of bacon permeated the restaurant, the bright sun shone in, and the summer sun was a little blinding through the big glass windows. We placed our orders, and while we waited for our food, I told Pat about contemplating going to the Fletcher School of Law and Diplomacy to find a vision for peace, and to try to make the world a better place.

He sat back in the booth, surprised. "Aren't you doing enough already?" he asked, but he didn't give me time to reply before adding, "Saint Thomas, my friend, you have received a calling. It was no coincidence that I read "Blessed be the Peacemakers" in my Bible devotional this morning before I came to meet with you."

Pat told me that he was very familiar with the Fletcher School at Tufts University and its longstanding reputation for academic excellence. I told him that the Fletcher School would be a big stretch for me, considering my age and limited financial resources. He was empathetic—specially around the financial challenges for my family. He zeroed in on that aspect of my decision, and asked if my father, my in-laws, or my siblings could help. I told him no, that I was on my own in that regard—but that I was giving thought to seeking help from friends and borrowing a significant amount of money.

After my meeting with Pat Albright, I sought advice and counsel from my friend and mentor, Bill Markus. I shared with Bill what I described as the *opening* I'd experienced, telling him that I wanted to know his thoughts before I proceeded to apply for admission. He enthusiastically embraced the idea, and encouraged me to go ahead.

I then shared the gist of these discussions with Phyllis, and told her I was going to apply for admission. She again expressed her opposition, but repeated that she was not going to worry about something that had only a remote possibility of becoming a reality.

I submitted my application for the academic year from July 2009 to July 2010, and immediately received a reply that my application was on a waiting list. Over the ensuing months, I kept in close touch with Nicki Sass—but as May 2009 rolled around, I became extremely anxious, knowing that a decision on my application had to be made by the end of May.

On the afternoon of Friday, May 15, I was working on my computer in my office when an email arrived. The sun was shining into my office from the side window, adjacent to my desk; I was engrossed in my work, and not expecting the email.

It was from Nicki, with a subject line that read "Congratulations!"

It brought tears to my eyes, and I said, "Oh my God, I got in!" I immediately called Nicki to thank her. I would be one of a class of thirty-five students—no matter if I had been the last person admitted! I knew God was at work—though I was later told that Nicki had also played a huge part in my getting accepted into the program. She'd really gone to bat for me.

I immediately called Phyllis to share the news. She was traveling with a friend, and I was able to reach her by cell phone while she was in the car driving. She reacted with the words, "That's great … if we don't go broke." Her tone was flat, almost a monotone; she was anything but enthusiastic. I knew at that moment that it was going to be an uphill struggle to get her on board. But I could also see that there was more to her reaction than financial concern—that she was masking her own fear of the unknown. Where was this going to lead me, and how would that affect her?

An important part of this difference was that Phyllis and I came from polar-opposite backgrounds, economically speaking. I came from a very modest, arguably sometimes poor, family, whereas Phyllis came from an affluent one. After we were married, she had a very hard time adjusting to her life with me, without financial security. She often said to me, "You just don't understand how hard this is, considering where I came from." It had been very hard for her to leave a comfortable home where she had never had a job, never had any financial responsibilities. I had started working as a caddy when I was thirteen years old; I'd worked, saved money, paid my way through college, bought my own car. I had learned the value of a dollar. Her life had been very different.

From the beginning, I'd assumed all the financial responsibilities in our marriage, from paying the bills to balancing the checkbook, securing mortgage financing, paying for our children's college education, and saving for retirement. Phyllis was glad to turn everything over to me, and I was accustomed to having those responsibilities. We always discussed financial decisions together, and learned to compromise. She always relied on my judgment, though she was often frustrated by my extreme caution with financial matters.

For my Fletcher School adventure, I developed a financial plan and presented it to Phyllis, just as I had done in so many instances before. It had always worked in the past. Fifteen years earlier, for example, I had gone out on my own and started my CPA practice without any income stream, without any cash reserves, and while taking on fifty thousand dollars of debt that included a third mortgage on our home. Those financial challenges caused a lot of bitterness and turmoil in our relationship—the financial uncertainty was easy for me to deal with due to my upbringing, but hard for Phyllis to accept. It took a toll on her emotional and physical health. Still, over time I showed her how I could navigate those treacherous waters to keep our family afloat—and our marriage survived that enormous stress test.

This time it was different. Phyllis did not buy into my plan.

The plan included my taking out a $40,000 student loan. I showed her how the loan would be paid over ten years, and that the monthly payment was equivalent to only two billable hours each month. It was certainly attainable, and the loan would be forgiven if I died or became disabled, ensuring that she would not be liable for it. The other part of my plan included seeking financial sponsorships from family, friends, and members of our church community—who were accustomed to supporting education for ministry—to pay the $22,500 tuition balance.

This was too much uncertainty for Phyllis. To her it just did not make sense for me to borrow $40,000 and enroll in a graduate program without a concrete outcome in sight. I told her that I was driven by the vision, with the hope that a tangible plan would emerge from my studies at the Fletcher School. I told her that this was why I was going to the Fletcher School in the first place—to pursue my vision.

These words made absolutely no sense to her. She told me this was so out of character for me, to be flying by the seat of my pants while taking on so much debt. (She wasn't wrong there.) She was also appalled that I would go out and ask for financial help from family, friends, and the church community to help pay my tuition; she worried about what other people would think. I explained to her that this was an example of the "Grand Gift Exchange"—the idea that we are all placed on this planet to help one another. And I would be asking for help to pay for my tuition, not for my own profit. I intended to use the knowledge I acquired at the Fletcher School to launch a ministry, to make the world a better place—a simple exchange of gifts. She didn't buy into this proposition, either.

But I went forward with my plan anyway.

The Fletcher School required a $5,000 deposit upon acceptance. I had already lined up sponsors to cover $4,500 of it; and to make the required deposit, I drew down $500 from our home equity line of credit. Then I was able to obtain my planned-for $40,000 in federal student loans, and the school would allow me to pay off the balance due over the next twelve months, before graduation. This would give me time to raise additional money through financial sponsorships.

I then visited our friend Tom Miller at his office on the north side of Pittsburgh. Over the thirty-four years I had known him, I'd never asked him for help. But my hope was that he would provide the bedrock of the financial sponsorships.

I'd first met Tom in the fall of 1974. He was Kathleen Rooney's boyfriend, and would later become her husband. Phyllis, Kathleen, and Mary Malia (those three Fontbonne girls I'd met on October 21, 1972) all attended Bethany College together. They were inseparable—going back to their freshman year in high school at Fontbonne Academy. Tom Miller and I soon became lifelong friends as well.

When I visited him it was a bright sunny morning, with the sunshine beaming into his office. Tom's desk was covered in scattered papers and stacks of documents—the normal state of affairs for him. But his mind was razor-sharp, organized, very analytical. He retained data easily, and was the smartest businessman I ever worked with. He always questioned my financial statements—"How can this be?" he would say—and we would go into drawn-out discussions of what made up the numbers. At the end of each round of these aggravating discussions, he always put forth his predictable question: "If we're making so much money, where's all of the cash?" After that, we'd both laugh and go on our way.

That morning, I found Tom at his desktop computer, immersed in his work. "The numbers look quite good," he said, still staring at the computer. He was only half-listening when I told him that I'd been accepted to the Fletcher School.

Continuing to gaze at the computer screen, he told me he wasn't surprised. I knew he would continue to half-listen unless I said something to grab his attention, so I said, "I need your help."

He stopped everything and sat up straight in his chair, his eyes focused on my eyes.

I said, "I need twelve thousand dollars to help me cover the cost of the Fletcher tuition." When he didn't say anything, I began to nervously explain the mechanics and the logistics of how he might deduct it as a business expense. There was a brief, very awkward moment of silence. Then he smiled at me.

"Sure," he said. "Sounds good."

That was all he said—he didn't ask a single question. It was a most welcome aberration from our normal lengthy discourse. I must say, without exaggeration, that I felt Kathleen's spirit in that brief meeting that day. Another angel who had interceded in my life, in this Fletcher journey, she was there supporting me. I thanked Tom and walked out of his office, taking a deep sigh of relief.

I remain eternally grateful for Tom's—and Kathleen's—help. He had lived up to the words he had written in an autograph book at the ten-year anniversary celebration of my CPA practice on May 23, 2004: *"When you get to a point in life when it is time to pause and reflect on the past, present, and future, the one thing that endures all are friends."*

———

After I met with Tom, I sent a letter to a select number of church members—members who I thought of as pillars of the church. The letter and follow-up conversations yielded dismal results. They all rejected my plea. One person told me I should take out a second mortgage on my home to finance this education expense. When I told her that I already had a second mortgage, she told me, "Then take out a third mortgage!"

After receiving those rejections I was sitting in my office, full of discouragement. I began to doubt myself, thinking, *Have I bitten off more than I can chew? Am I unrealistically idealistic?* Just then, out of the blue, I received a telephone call from Walt Heintzleman.

I had met Walt Heintzleman and his wife Lynn through my church's Bible study. Walt and I had also served on the church's Board of Trustees and a subcommittee that oversaw the renovation and construction of a $1 million bell-tower at the church, aptly named the Peace Tower.

After his call, I would realize that Walt was God's messenger, calling with a message that really lifted me up. He began the conversation by saying, "Tom, I'd like to share a story with you, if you have the time. But before I do that, I want you to know that Lynn and I will contribute a thousand dollars towards your Fletcher School education expense." Oh, I welcomed those kind words!

Walt and I spoke for close to an hour that day, and he shared with me his own faith journey. Several years before that day, Walt and Lynn had made a conscious, purposeful commitment to make Jesus Christ the center of their lives—not just in word, but in action as well. Their commitment drove their actions related to family, vocation, and community. Now, it was evident to me that he and Lynn were fulfilling their commitment by supporting me. They were walking their talk.

Just a few days after I met with Tom and spoke with Walt, Pat Albright telephoned me to check in. He invited me to meet with him for another breakfast meeting, and I shared my progress with him. He offered to write an endorsement letter to the entire congregation to ask for help. He would personally sign the letter, on the church's letterhead. I felt the presence of God in our midst—a warm, tingling, and comforting sensation throughout my entire body.

Pat would later tell me that he got some pushback from some of the higher-ups in the church, but he went against the grain and proceeded anyway. This is the content of his letter:

In over fifty years as an ordained clergyman, I have shared experiences of a great many people who have received a "call from on High." My friend, Tom Etzel, has felt that summons. I have known Tom for over five years as a good friend and a student in the Bible class that I teach at Southminster Presbyterian Church. As an idealist of the highest order, Tom seeks to discern practical ways of putting the gospel into practice and use. Needless to say, he is doing this at great cost to the Etzel family.

Tom's plan of action involves a Global Master of Arts program (GMAP) at the Fletcher School of Law and Diplomacy, at Tufts University in the Boston area. I was very aware of the school during my graduate studies at Boston University. GMAP entails high-intensity course work, enriching internet-mediated studies, and multiple weeks of residency at the university and abroad. Admission to this program was very selective.

With this program, Tom will be preparing for a global peace and justice ministry. This will allow him to explore areas for ministry in promoting peace and justice world-wide.

GMAP has various demands, one being the high economic cost of over $62,500. It is my earnest prayer that many of us would help Tom in this endeavor. After all, he will be preparing to be our minister-missionary in a field that needs us all.

Pat's appeal bore fruit, and his grassroots-level campaign filled the gap. It was quite powerful. I received many notes with words of encouragement and support. I knew that many people were praying for me, and Pat continued to support me with his prayers, interest, and encouragement throughout the academic year.

―――――

Phyllis never quite got on board with me going to the Fletcher School. There was just too much uncertainty for her, and I didn't have answers to her questions:

What are you going to do with this degree?

How are you going to pay for it?

How are you going to take this on and at the same time run your practice?

What do you intend to do after you complete the program?

Don't you think that you're being self-centered?

Isn't your family more important than making the world a better place?

With this last question, her tone seemed a bit sarcastic—but it was a valid question that most people would ask.

Nonetheless, I went ahead, even though I knew my decision was going to be a source of great discord between us. This decision was emotionally driven—it honored my Scorpio side, just as Mwezi Mtoto had recommended. I was propelled forward by the opening—by a force beyond my control, a power greater than myself. It was the first time in my life with Phyllis that she and I did not find a common ground: I didn't compromise or give in, and she remained steadfast. Prior to this moment, we had always held each other close, wrapped our arms around each other in times of joy (the births of Kristen, Katie, and Mark) and despair (the deaths of Kathleen, Isy, Katie McCloskey, and my mother and sister). We had always stuck together and dealt with life's challenges as a team.

This time was different. I felt all alone. It felt as though my wife, partner, and best friend had let go of my hand and turned back while I was walking into a pitch-black forest in the middle of the night. And I know that Phyllis was experiencing the same lonely feeling—that she felt abandoned by me as I walked away.

There was no light as I entered those woods, not even a glimmer of moonlight peeking through the trees. The wind started to kick up, and leaves on the ground swirled around my feet. I crept slowly along in the dark. But I remembered that the darkest hour is just before the dawn. And as I walked, I became full of hope that dawn was just around the corner to shed a brilliant light on my path. And inside me, I felt a resilient faith that I would find my way, just as I had done so many times before in my life.

I knew that the journey I was about to begin was going to be hard, the way it is supposed to be. And I plowed full-steam ahead.

———

CHAPTER TWELVE

A Brand-new World

The Fletcher School GMAP first term started in July 2009. The month of July was designated as a reading period, and I received several boxes via FedEx, full of books and articles. Reality set in: I was officially starting my one-year GMAP studies.

Included in the mailing was a syllabus and reading list for each course for the first term: Leadership and Management, International Negotiation, International Finance, and International Politics. I devoted my early morning hours to reading to try to get through it all. The International Politics class required the most reading, but all of it was challenging; I never had so much required reading in my undergraduate studies or my brief stint in graduate school. This was the beginning of a new challenge: balancing my time between running my CPA practice and the Fletcher School's academic demands. It was a new source of stress in my life.

I read the book *Getting to Yes: Negotiating Agreement Without Giving In*, by Roger Fisher, in its entirety for the International Negotiation course. While reading the book, I noticed that Diana Chigas, one of the professors for the course, was cited in the book. She had worked with the author at the Harvard Negotiation Project. I was impressed that Professor Chigas was such an authority in the field.

My main takeaway from all this reading was that the profound value of individualism, individual rights, and individual freedom was at the core of American culture. This was contrasted to how many other places in the world, especially in Africa, have more of a sense of community or collective values embedded in their cultures. I would later learn how individualism can be a detriment to altruism, the principle or practice of unselfish concern for or devotion to the welfare of others—how individualism can be a detriment to the greater good.

Soon it was time for my first on-campus residency. My flight was unfortunately cancelled, so I caught a Monday-morning flight and hailed a taxi to the Tufts University campus in Medford, Massachusetts.

I arrived around noon, at the dormitory building. I remembered walking past this dormitory building with Nicki Sass during my visit a year before. I hurriedly checked in at the receptionist desk, got my keys, and lugged my bags upstairs to my dorm room. It was a three-bedroom suite with a kitchen, a bathroom, and a living room with chairs and a couch, and it was clear that my suitemates had already settled in.

The receptionist gave me a campus map and pointed me in the direction of the Fletcher School. I was in such a hurry that I jogged, even in the sweltering heat—wearing a suit and tie and carrying a briefcase. It felt as if I were rushing through the airport to catch a flight.

I found the lecture hall empty, and figured everyone must be at lunch. A woman walked in as I was looking around trying to make sense of it all, and introduced herself as Rebecca Crispin. She was friendly, welcoming, and had a calm way about her. She reassured me that I was in the right place, and that our classmates were still at lunch. Rebecca told me that she was a military officer in the United States Army, in her final GMAP term. She told me that the Fletcher School was a good place and that I would enjoy my time there, and directed me to the Mugar Café, where the rest of our class was having lunch.

It was toward the tail end of the lunch hour by the time I arrived at the Mugar Café, and I was too nervous to eat. Two classmates, Scott

Tully from Boston and Mayuresh Kulkarni from India, welcomed me to a table. I began to feel comfortable as I spoke with them. Scott told me he'd played football at Yale with a couple of guys from Upper St. Clair, a suburb south of Pittsburgh that neighbored Mt. Lebanon.

We had barely completed our introductions when it was time to return to the lecture hall. When I got up from the table, Salman Al Farisi, a diplomat from Indonesia, came and introduced himself and told me that we were suitemates.

By the time I returned to the lecture hall, most of my classmates were already settled into their seats. I stood at the entrance for a quick moment to take in the grand amphitheater-style lecture hall. One of my classmates, Juan Monge from Costa Rica, later told me that when he saw me standing there, he thought I was one of the professors! I must have fit the stereotype of a professor—beard, suit, and tie, with a briefcase.

Most of the seats were already taken, but I noticed an open one at the very top row. On my way in, many of my classmates got up and introduced themselves. I noticed that for many, English was not their native language. It dawned on me that I had never experienced such a friendly and welcoming group of people in all my formal and professional continuing education. This felt good.

When I got to the top, I sat down between a woman who introduced herself as May Salameh and another woman named Layla Ferguson. Both women were probably two decades younger than me. After I got settled, the GMAP technology person walked up the steps to my row and handed me my new laptop computer. I opened it, but did not know how to turn it on. I asked the technology person to come back and tell me how to turn it on. I could see that both May and Layla were staring at me, and imagined that they were thinking to themselves, *Oh wow, this old man is going to need a lot of help!*

May was very outgoing and amusing with her frequent comments during class. She had the entire class howling. She was most worried about her internet connection not working when she returned to Yemen. She kept saying, "I'll be stranded in the middle of the desert, and I won't be able to connect with anyone!"

Layla, by contrast, was quiet and shy. During a break in the afternoon lecture, I leaned over toward her and whispered, "Your first name is one of my favorite songs." She looked at me, broke into a huge smile, and said, "Oh my God, I get that all of the time, especially at the airport check-in counters!" She told me she was a California girl, and that her parents had been hippies. I shared with her that I had recently been to Bethel, New York, the site of the 1969 Woodstock music festival. This caught Layla's attention; she wanted to hear all about it. For a moment, my mind drifted back to August 1969, to the festival held on Max Yasgur's dairy farm in Bethel. The concert promoters had expected a crowd of 50,000 … and 500,000 had showed up. It was a phenomenon never to be replicated—and the fact that 500,000 people had gathered for three days of peace and music, found their collective voices through the music and lyrics without one violent incident, still seems incredible to me.

But our conversation ended abruptly as the professor began her lecture.

———

That first afternoon made a lasting impression on me. You could feel the energy in the room—there was much discussion among the students and interaction with Anna Seleny, our International Politics professor. It was a lively and energized group of professionals, eager to learn. The only concern I had at the end of that class was that Professor Seleny kept referring to the discussion boards, a.k.a. "the boards." I had no idea what she was talking about. This would turn out to be one of the technology challenges I would have to face, far beyond learning how to turn on my laptop.

At the end of the afternoon classes, I returned to the dormitory to unpack and get settled in. That was when I met my other suite-mate, Steve Lord, who lived in the Hudson Valley in New York and worked in the financial-services industry on Wall Street. Steve was genuinely friendly and very humble—not the stereotyped competitive Wall Street financial type. This was refreshing to me. Throughout our GMAP year together, Steve was there to help me.

I also re-met Salman Al Farisi, our third suitemate whom I'd met briefly at lunch. He was very friendly and polite and had a great sense of humor. Salman, Steve, and I barely had enough time to get acquainted before we were off to the cocktail reception scheduled on the lawn outside of Ballou Hall, which I learned was Tufts's first academic building, built in 1852.

Before we left the dormitory, we weren't sure how to dress. The itinerary said to dress in business attire, so we wore suits and ties to be on the safe side. When we arrived, we saw that the men wore suits and ties like us, and the women wore bright, colorful summer dresses. The weather was perfect for an outdoor reception on the campus lawn. It was bright and sunny, a gorgeous summer evening. I really enjoyed going around and meeting more of my classmates. Our class was loud and full of enthusiasm and excitement.

Dean Nutter made it a point to come over to me to say hello and extend a warm welcome to the Fletcher School, as did the GMAP administrative staff—Nicki Sass, Emma Heffern, Marni Powers, and Endri Misho. A congenial spirit permeated the air at the reception that initial evening that would only get stronger as the year progressed.

After the reception, we were ushered into Ballou Hall for a formal sit-down dinner. This historic building was purposely chosen, bridging the Fletcher School tradition to the new, innovative GMAP approach.

The seating prearranged us into teams. This team approach, we soon learned, was the cornerstone of GMAP. Throughout our studies, both on campus and when we returned home to continue learning remotely, we could rely on our peers to provide guidance and assistance. As I sat down, I had my first glimpse of my five teammates: Jim Ayres (United States), Tam Le (Vietnam), Sylvia Cabrera (Mexico), Patricia Clarke (Grenada), and Mayuresh Kulkarni (India).

Dean Nutter started the dinner with a toast to the GMAP Class of 2010. She then delivered an inspirational speech covering the history and traditions of the Fletcher School, of GMAP, and of the Fletcher Community. In 1933, the Fletcher School of Law and Diplomacy had been founded as the first graduate-only school of international affairs in the United States, thanks to Dr. Austin Fletcher's one-million-dollar donation. He'd envisioned the school as a beacon of hope in a time of despair.

One notable initiative that had emerged from the Fletcher School was the Global Master of Arts Program (GMAP), spearheaded by Dean Nutter. In 2000, GMAP was introduced with a unique purpose: utilizing future technology to provide the Fletcher experience to students who were unable to participate in a full-time residency program.

Upon graduation from the Fletcher School, we would join the ranks of the Fletcher Community, an expansive network of leaders, innovators, and changemakers spanning the globe. This interconnected community would serve as a valuable resource, enabling us to make a significant impact in our respective fields and contribute to positive change worldwide.

Dean Nutter promised that the entire GMAP staff and faculty

were there to support us, to do everything in their power to ensure our success. I sensed that Dean Nutter was committed to maintaining GMAP's reputation of academic excellence. She was a trailblazer, and I sat there in awe, feeling very honored to be given the opportunity to study at this institution.

Dean Nutter ended her speech with a quote from Winston Churchill: "Never, never, never give up!" It turned out that this was Dean Nutter's mantra, and she would use it to cheer us on for the entire academic year.

I had a hard time sleeping that first night, after such an action-packed first day of the residency. But I soon learned that it had just been a warm-up.

My days started at the crack of dawn as I pulled myself out of bed and sprinted to the shower before Salman and Steve got up. I would then check my emails for my CPA practice to stay in touch with my clients, and was usually the first to arrive at the Mugar Café for coffee and a hearty breakfast. This gave me a good opportunity to casually chat with my classmates and get to know them better.

The remainder of each day followed a regimented schedule of lectures and brief breaks. During coffee breaks in and around the Mugar Café, I listened to my classmates speaking many different languages, including French, Spanish, and Arabic. (The café also had a generous supply of chocolate candies, my favorite.) Our daily lectures were followed by an hour or so of free time before we convened for a catered dinner in the dormitory dining hall.

During that first week, time was also devoted to an introduction to the Fletcher School's Library Resources, Career Services, and Office of Development and Alumni Relations. We had a brief session instructing us on how to read efficiently—how to skim and scan to get the gist of an article without having to read every single word. (I chuckled to myself that I could have applied this skill back when I was an undergraduate.) Each team also participated in an exercise or game to teach us how to spot cultural differences and varying customs. All the members of my team thought that this was an important learning tool for us at this early stage of our year together; it helped us to be mindful of differences, and to better understand and accept each other.

We were introduced to Nicholas Kenney, our thesis instructor, and were handed *The Craft of Research*. Nick, a doctoral candidate at the Fletcher School, would work with us from our proposal to our final thesis, and help us prepare for our thesis presentation.

We were also assigned a team project to develop that would be presented to faculty members and our classmates on Friday, the final day of the first residency. This turned out to be a good team-building process. Our team spent evenings and some time during the days preparing our presentation on the effects of climate change. We pulled together, and our team began to gel. There was no jockeying for power; we all wanted to work together to succeed. We were building mutual trust and respect.

It became apparent that I was immersed in a program built around exceptional students with a common thread: open mindedness combined with intellectual curiosity. And GMAP had an international emphasis—just what the Fletcher School had promised.

By the time the first week ended, I was exhausted. I felt that I had gone through a week of boot camp. On Friday night our class went on a dinner cruise along the St. Charles River, and Saturday was our first day of free time. I spent the morning getting better acquainted with my laptop computer, the discussion board, and the overall technology platform. In the afternoon, my teammate Patricia and I took a leisurely walk down to Davis Square, and then on Saturday night, a small group of us hopped on the subway to Cambridge to a salsa dance studio. Our classmate Franco, from Peru, was an exceptional dancer. I loved watching him dance—he was so good that a line of women formed, waiting patiently to get their turn to dance with him.

On Sunday afternoon we hopped on a bus to go to a traditional New England lobster bake on Cape Cod. This was a brand-new experience for me. One of the Fletcher professors opened his house to us, and we spent the afternoon and evening eating fine New England food and getting to know each other better. I had great fun, and by the time we returned to campus it was pitch-dark and time for bed.

***

CHAPTER THIRTEEN
The Second Week

The schedule for week two of the residency was more rigorous than that of the first week. In addition to our daily lecture schedule, the deadline for our team project on climate change was rapidly approaching. I kept urging my team to have a Skype rehearsal session—they all knew how to use Skype, but I didn't. Skype was the virtual tool we would use to communicate with our team members scattered all over the globe, and I was worried about going home and being stranded without knowing how to use it. To top it off, I was having difficulty grasping the concepts in the International Finance lectures (too many graphs for me).

All these worries came to a head by midweek. It happened early in the morning while I was in the shower. I stood under the shower head while the hot water poured over my head. My arms were outstretched and pressed against the shower wall, and I felt myself overcome with fear and anxiety. I began to ask myself, *Have I taken on more than I can handle? How am I going to keep this pace? My brain is already exhausted; how am I going to do this for a whole year? Is the technology too much for me? Will I ever figure out how to navigate the boards? How am I ever going to get through tax season with this additional workload? Am I crazy, spending all this money without even knowing what I'm going to do with this degree? Will I find my vision? Maybe Phyllis was right!*

But then I took a step back. *Now wait a minute,* I thought. *I have already faced many hurdles and bumps in the road up to this point in my life. There is no reason why I can't rise to this challenge! This will be a walk in the park compared to what I faced when I started my CPA practice, from scratch, when I was forty years old!*

With these thoughts, I pulled myself together. I became determined not to give in to fear and emerged from the shower feeling strong and determined. As the second week progressed, my fears began to dissipate.

My favorite course in the GMAP first term was International Negotiation. I sat in the lecture hall listening to Professor Diana Chigas's presentation about how diplomacy takes place across different levels of society, sometimes referred to as "tracks" in the academic world, and in the peace building field. She defined the three tracks as follows:

Track One: Top-level diplomacy by governmental or intergovernmental organizations. Examples include the United Nations, the Organization for Security and Cooperation in Europe, and the African Union.

Track Two: Mid-level diplomacy by civil society organizations and prominent individuals. An example is former President Jimmy Carter in North Korea in 1994.

Track Three: Diplomacy at the grassroots or local community level. This track focuses on long-term relationship-building among ordinary citizens.

In Professor Chigas's presentation on these three tracks, the Track Three level caught my eye, with several pictures of ordinary citizens engaged in peace building. This segment took only a few minutes. But it turned out to be the most important few minutes of my entire GMAP year. Up to that point, I never knew that ordinary citizens were involved in peace building at the grassroots level. This was the catalyst that helped me find my way.

My first gut reaction was, *Hmm, this is done by ordinary citizens, at the grassroots level. I bet this is something that I could do.* I didn't experience an epiphany, and definitely not an "opening" when Professor Chigas introduced me to Track Three diplomacy—it was more like a discovery, an awakening, a coming into awareness. But in the long run, it proved to be monumental for me. That little tidbit of information that Professor Chigas introduced me to would ultimately help me find my path toward what I initially described—harkening back to Pat Albright's letter on my behalf to our church community—as my *global peace and justice ministry.*

Still, I must admit that on an intellectual level, skepticism quickly set in. I began to think, *How can ordinary citizens make a difference? Isn't this type of work for government—for big organizations like the U.N.—for famous, influential people? Aren't bigger organizations better suited for this type of work?*

There was a whole lot more for me to learn about and delve into. I needed to dig deeper—and the Fletcher GMAP contagion of intellectual curiosity began to affect me.

————

Our team held a "rehearsal Skype meeting" one evening in the dining hall. We had fun with it and laughed uncontrollably at moments as our voices echoed throughout the dining hall. I learned that using Skype wasn't so hard after all.

One of my GMAP classmates, Juliana Magalhaes, came up to me after the final International Finance lecture on Thursday afternoon and offered to help me via Skype. She could sense that I had been pretty much clueless as I'd raised my hand with many questions during our professor's lectures. Juliana, originally from Brazil, was now living in Bangkok, and her act of kindness allayed my worries. And she did follow up on her offer. She and I would speak frequently via Skype, and she shared with me all her copious notes from our on-campus lectures and remote video lessons.

On Thursday evening, Dean Nutter invited our GMAP class to her home for cocktails and dinner. It was a boisterous affair as we celebrated getting through our first residency. We were so loud and exuberant that even the dean could not bring calm to the disarray. She told me she would normally say a few words, but on this evening, under the circumstances, she punted. She didn't want to disrupt the party.

During the party, my teammates began to affectionly call me "the dean" because of my age. Tam, my teammate from Vietnam, pulled me aside and told me, "Tom, I admire you." When I asked him why he'd said such a nice thing, he replied, "Because you are so old!" I thanked him, and he and I cracked up. He then said, with tears in his eyes, "Tom, I consider you a friend. You are always welcome to come visit me in Vietnam." He touched my heart. I thanked him again, and promised him that I would take him up on his offer.

On Friday, our team-project presentation on climate change— held in front of our entire GMAP class and faculty—went well, despite the combative comments and questioning from one of the professors, who to me seemed pompous and disrespectful. From the expression on some of the other professors' faces, they seemed to think the same—but I was determined not to let him intimidate me.

The team-project presentation was our final act for the two-week residency, and afterward my classmates and I quickly dispersed and headed to the airport. I was glad to go back home. The first residency had seemed like a whole lot longer than two weeks—a whole new world had opened up to me.

When I left campus that Friday evening, it was with a feeling of connectedness to my team, to my GMAP class, and to the Fletcher School. I was in the right place. The sense of belonging to a community had begun to sink in.

———

CHAPTER FOURTEEN
Internet Learning

After the initial two-week residency, GMAP gave us a week off. I welcomed this respite, although I had a lot of catching up to do in my CPA practice; I was excited to go home to see Phyllis and the kids.

On Saturday morning, Phyllis, Mark, and I sat down at the dining-room table and looked through the GMAP class directory, with pictures of my classmates. They were both impressed with the diversity of the class, and I shared more details about a few of my teammates with them:

Jim Ayres, with a master's degree in business (MBA), was the executive director of a non-profit organization in western Massachusetts. He'd instantly become the leader of our team, and we welcomed his willingness to take on this important role.

Tam Le, like me, had a financial background: he was an investment banker. He had a master's degree from the Massachusetts Institute of Technology (MIT), and he later shared that when he was a child in Vietnam, he had walked through rice paddies to get to school and read by the light of a kerosene lamp because his home didn't have electricity.

Sylvia Cabrera, a diplomat from Mexico, had another graduate degree as well as a juris doctorate degree. She possessed extraordinary writing skills.

Patricia Clarke was a diplomat from Grenada. Like Sylvia, she was an excellent writer. Her verbal communication skills were extraordinary—her delivery was so fluid, so smooth. Patricia's laid-back Caribbean appearance was deceiving, as she brought an intensity to her work and studies.

Mayuresh Kulkarni, in the technology field, was from India and now working in Sweden. He spoke about our team projects as "deliverables," using technology jargon. His parents were teachers, and he had come to the United States without knowing how to speak a single word of English. He told us that he'd learned to speak English by watching reruns of *I Love Lucy*.

Mark was excited for me, and he commented that he had never seen me so passionate. His observation was in line with Mwezi Mtoto's claim that my emotional side had been oppressed throughout most of my life, and I realized that for the most part, throughout Mark's young life I'd kept my nose to the grindstone working. He was only six years old when I'd started my CPA practice. Sixteen years had passed by, and now he was witnessing a more vibrant me. I was exuberant—and it showed. His acknowledgment of the passion that had laid dormant in me for so many years made me happy. For her part, Phyllis was reticent, but also showed interest. That made me feel good too. It was a big step in our healing process.

Our internet-mediated learning began a week later on the morning of Sunday, August 23, 2009, when our team held its first Skype call: seven a.m. for me in Pittsburgh, and six in the evening for Tam in Vietnam. Our team calls were scheduled for every Sunday morning from then until the end of the term in December. I had requested this time slot so I could attend my Sunday-morning Bible study at my church; I knew I needed that community experience both to stay grounded, and for support and spiritual nourishment.

Attendance at the team Skype calls was mandatory, and essential to the success of the remote learning. Each member of our team took turns to be the call leader, in charge of initiating the call, organizing the agenda, running the meeting, and keeping us on track. This team approach involved many team projects—or "deliverables," as Mayuresh would say—that had to be planned, executed, and completed on time. Throughout each week, we stayed in close contact via email. Communication was critical, and our team did an excellent job with it, despite our work demands. We shared a tremendous spirit of commitment and cooperation.

When I first logged in, the GMAP discussion board was intimidating to me. I was overwhelmed by the sheer quantity of the posts, the quality of the writing, and the length and depth of the threaded discussions. I felt like I was the last horse out of the gate in the Kentucky Derby: all the other horses were galloping forward, headed to the first turn, while I was just a few yards past the opening gate, slogging along. Everything was moving quickly, and I felt way behind, overwhelmed.

This has happened to me many times in my education experience. I have always been a slow learner—my brain processes things slowly. This has always made it more difficult for me to grasp new concepts. My entire education, from elementary school all the way through college, required a struggle for me to keep up.

Too intimidated to make a single post on the discussion board the first week, I simply read and absorbed others' words. My teammates noticed my absence. During our second team meeting, my teammate Patricia voiced her concern, and encouraged me to make that first post. I literally spent at least two hours crafting a three-paragraph post, then asked my daughter Kristen to show me how to upload it to the discussion board on the platform. It took Kristen just a few minutes to give me the instructions to copy and paste the post from

Word to the platform. "Dad, I'm worried about you," she said. "You need to speed it up."

"Oh yes, I've heard that comment before," I said. "It's been the story of my life!"

Kristen showed me the way, and it wasn't so scary after all. But I always say, "It's easy when you know what you're doing"—and how cool it was that my twenty-six-year-old daughter, having completed both her undergraduate degree in elementary education and her graduate degree as a reading specialist, was now teaching me, a soon-to-be-fifty-five-year-old graduate-school student!

I made that first post just before our family Sunday dinner, in response to one of Professor Chigas's discussion questions. I was anxious all through dinner to check for feedback, and after dinner I sprinted up the two flights of steps to my home office and logged in. Discovering that Professor Chigas had replied to my post, I was delighted by her positive response—she agreed with most of my positions. What a relief! I'd done it!

The first time is always the hardest, and once I'd made that first posting, I was well on my way. Even with my slow start, I finished strong on the boards by the end of the term in December.

The activity on the boards occupied quite a bit of time. In addition, early in the term, Professor Chigas presented us with an innovative learning project called the Quota Case. This project was a hypothetical negotiation scenario involving a fishing dispute in the Atlantic Ocean off the coast of North America, with our team negotiating with another GMAP team. This gave us a sense of what it would be like to negotiate with a foreign adversary. I represented our team on a special Skype call. The other GMAP team was represented by Bujar Hoxha from Kosovo and Michael Kunz from the U.S. The call seemed real because of Bujar's accent; I sensed from the beginning of the call that these two gentlemen were skilled negotiators. I learned from this exercise that you must compromise so that each side wins, and that you need to build trust and respect to reach a settlement.

In addition to the video lectures, discussion boards, and team projects, there were individual writing assignments, many of which required much research and critical thinking.

One of these was a negotiation analysis paper, for which we could choose our own topic. My paper was "Potential Peace Negotiations: The United States and the Taliban in Afghanistan," a hypothetical negotiation scenario. I acted as the National Security Advisor to President Obama. At the time, there was little evidence, if any, that talks or any type of reconciliation process had occurred to date. This scenario was of special interest to me because of 9/11, and the link between the Al Qaeda terrorist attack on the U.S. and the Taliban's presence in Afghanistan. Eight years had passed since 9/11, yet the United States continued to surround itself with superficial borders, embroiled in an endless quagmire. I chose to cross that border, reach out to the adversary, and seek a peaceful reconciliation. The analysis set forth several factors that supported the strong possibility that the time might be ripe for talks to begin. Unfortunately, in real life it would take until 2020 for serious peace negotiations to take place between the United States, the Afghan government, and the Taliban.

Each of us also had the task of selecting a country to address its prospects for political and economic liberalization and, ultimately, democracy. I chose the West African country of Guinea; after reading some articles in *The New York Times*, I sensed that Guinea was on the cusp of a new era. I had known very little about Guinea, but quickly learned about its history of authoritarian rule for over fifty years and the death of its dictator, Lansana Conte, in 2008. His death had left a void in power that was quickly filled by a military junta, a small group ruling the country before a legally constituted government was instituted. But my hunch was that there was soon going to be a sudden change in the status quo.

As it turned out, power was handed over to a freely elected civilian administration in 2010. The news about Guinea's shift in power put a smile on my face—and reinforced my core belief in the power of the people that manifests in grassroots movements as they find their voice together, become empowered, and bring about change.

———

CHAPTER FIFTEEN
Unexpected Takeaways

At 9:31 p.m. on December 31, 2009, I was on a flight to Lisbon, Portugal. The Fletcher School always held its mid-year residency in an international location, and a GMAP alumnus who lived in that location help the GMAP staff select hotel accommodations and schedule speakers. The hotel and food expenses were included in our tuition, but we had to pay for our travel expenses.

This was my very first trip to Europe. A few hours into the flight the flight attendants began serving champagne, and the pilot soon led us in a toast by exclaiming, "Happy New Year!" A new year, a new decade, and a new adventure were upon me. I took a deep breath while I embraced the moment, pinching myself to make sure this was for real. I felt chills run up and down my body—and I said a little prayer as I counted my blessings.

It was early morning on New Year's Day when the plane touched down and I set foot in Lisbon. I was a bit nervous, not knowing what to expect from going through customs and security, getting to the hotel, not being able to speak Portuguese, and being jetlagged. I was glad to see a familiar face as I deplaned: Ruth Lande, a GMAP classmate, had been on the plane with me! Ruth, a much more experienced traveler, led the way.

Ruth and I made it without a glitch from the airport to the Sofitel Lisbon Hotel, located right smack in the middle of the city of Lisbon. The mid-year residency was scheduled to start on Sunday, January 3;

I'd purposely arrived in Lisbon a couple of days early to give myself a little bit of time to get over my jetlag and play tourist before the rigorous academic schedule kicked in. (Most importantly, I didn't want to be late again.) I was impressed with the professionalism of the hotel staff as I checked in, and relieved when I noticed that they all spoke English very well.

I quickly unpacked and got settled, and called Phyllis to let her know that I arrived safely. She had cried when I left to go to the Pittsburgh airport. She always worried when I traveled, especially after 9/11. The trauma from that day would forever stay with her, and her fear was compounded, given the fact that I was traveling such a long distance out of the country—all the way across the Atlantic Ocean to Europe. We both said how weird it was that we weren't together on New Year's Day, considering we had celebrated that holiday together for thirty-eight years! I missed her already.

Next, I called my GMAP classmate Juliana, who had told me to give her a call when I arrived. She and her husband Paulo were staying at their apartment in Cascais, located on the coastline to the west of Lisbon. She invited me and Ruth to their apartment for dinner that evening, and gave me directions on where to catch the train, which seemed easy enough.

Ruth and I took a long walk throughout the center of the city that afternoon. It was bright and sunny, a bit chilly, with many people out and about for New Year's Day. The mood was festive, with music playing in the spacious plaza in the center of the city. I must really have stuck out as an outsider in the crowd of people. Several beggars came up to me, even grabbing my arm and asking me for money. This was something I'd never experienced in the U.S.—and Ruth, in a protective manner, asked them to stop and move away from us.

I was struck by the historic monuments, some built as far back as the fifteenth century. The narrow streets and sidewalks were made of cobblestone and quite slippery. (After a few days into the residency, Juliana helped me buy Portuguese-made shoes with better traction.) Late in the afternoon, Ruth and I hopped on a train to get to Juliana's apartment. We had a little difficulty figuring out how to put money into the kiosk to buy the train tickets. A kind gentleman noticed that we were having trouble and showed us how—and we were able to communicate, even though Ruth and I didn't speak Portuguese, and he didn't speak English! His kind action spoke louder than words. It reinforced my belief that we, as human beings, are all placed on this earth to help one another as we interact at the grassroots level, doing things that seem to be insignificant but really make a big difference. Even language barriers can't undermine our common humanity.

We departed the train at the stop near Juliana's apartment, and saw her waiting for us. She literally jumped for joy when she saw us—we were all excited to see each other. It felt as though we were longtime childhood friends being reunited, even though we had only known each other for five months.

We had a lovely dinner with Juliana, Paulo, and their children. They were so friendly, welcoming, and engaging, and I felt at home with them. The connection Juliana and I had forged in our first term had expanded to her entire family, and I didn't feel alone or that far away from home, even considering that this was my first trip abroad. I had an inkling that perhaps somehow I could find a way to connect people on a global scale by expanding personal relationships, so that they would feel less alone in the world—just as I felt that evening.

By the time Juliana and Paulo drove us back to the hotel, I was glad to hit the sack. It had been quite a New Year's Day in Lisbon, and a great start to a new year and a new decade.

Several of my classmates began arriving the next day, so there was another reunion of sorts. We hung out in the hotel's restaurant, drinking coffee and catching up after the holiday break. Steve Lord, Ruth, Juliana, and I then took a stroll about the city, Juliana acting as our tour guide. She led us up a hill to the Castelo de Sao Jorge, once a Moorish castle that had become the home of Portuguese kings and was later transformed into a public garden with an observation terrace providing spectacular views over Lisbon and its bright, multicolored rooftops. We later stopped to have lunch together, gearing up for the mid-year residency about to begin the next day.

On Sunday morning, I got up extra early and headed down to the hotel café for breakfast. I was excited to chat with my classmates and catch up with those who'd arrived the night before. Right as we were ending breakfast and beginning to take a stroll down the hall towards the meeting room, May Salameh appeared at the café entrance. She had flown in late the night before from Amman, and I was glad to see her. She had confided in me during the holiday break that she had doubts about returning in January, and had thought about quitting the program. When she'd asked me for my thoughts, I'd told her that she would never have this opportunity again—that now was the time to finish the program, to get the degree. She'd heeded my advice and didn't quit. Seven months later, the night before we graduated, Dean Nutter told me that she thought that I was a giver, a quiet leader—and she believed that May would not have been graduating the next day had it not been for my support. May and I developed a lifelong friendship that transcended the superficial differences of age—May was in her late twenties—and ethnicity—May is a Muslim and Palestinian. She'd had extensive international living experience and is fluent in several languages: Arabic, English, Spanish, and French. All of this fascinated me. But most importantly, it was our common humanity that helped us endure the Fletcher School academic rigors.

This, more than anything, served as our bridge.

We were assigned to new teams in Lisbon. My new teammates were Ruth Lande (U.S.A.), Juan Monge (Costa Rica), Manish Pandey (Nepal), Beatriz Vergara (Canary Islands), and Bujar Hoxha (Kosovo). My new teammates were just as rich in talent, open-minded, and intellectually curious as my first ones had been. Ruth had twenty-plus years' experience in healthcare administration; Juan worked as an attorney with the United Nations; Beatriz had extensive experience in economic and business development and international trade (in both the public and private sectors); and Bujar and Manish held leadership positions in the NGO world, serving those in need.

My new team gelled quickly. We had some familiarity with each other by having read each other's postings on the first-term discussion boards. Bujar took the initiative to outline our individual lead assignments for some of the team projects, and we held our first team meeting in Lisbon and got off to a great start. I felt that I could make a significant contribution in the Global Finance course, considering my financial background. Bujar began to affectionately call me "Mr. President," and my new title, a step up from "the Dean" quickly spread throughout my GMAP class. I loved it.

———

Bujar helped me put in perspective that the struggles I'd experienced in my adolescent years were a walk in the park compared to his own life-threatening conflict-zone experience, and I began to appreciate more my good fortune of having grown up in Bethel Park. His story gave me a first-hand insight of a young person's trauma, and the images would remain in my mind's eye as I took steps to set up the GPBF to prevent other children and youth in the world experiencing the same horror Bujar had endured.

Every day in Lisbon was action-packed. All the professors flew in from Boston, which gave us the opportunity to spend time with them and have casual conversation over breakfast, lunch, and dinner. Our classes started at eight every morning, and lectures extended into many evenings as the GMAP team brought in speakers from the diplomatic world, many of whom were Fletcher School alumni.

One presentation stood out to me: one given by a U.S. foreign service officer, stationed in Portugal, who spoke about his career. He mentioned that his career had included a stint in Rwanda during the 1994 genocide in which eight hundred thousand Tutsis, the minority ethnic group, were slaughtered by armed militia in three months. I asked if he'd seen it coming. He said, "Well, we really blew that one. We didn't have a clue."

I wondered, *How can that be—you're living and working in a country, and you aren't in tune with the underlying tension about to explode? There must be a better way.*

Years later I read that one warning sign of an impending genocide is severe political, economic, or religious discrimination against minorities. Feeling oppressed, without a voice, people may turn to violence—as even my father had, in that shocking episode from

Bujar Hoxha

Bujar Hoxha and I met at the Fletcher School in 2010, sharing a table at brunch in between GMAP classes. Despite coming from two very different worlds, we instantly hit it off. We negotiated against each other in a class exercise later that week and reached a compromise, a clear sign to me that we would work well together.

Then he and I were assigned to the same team for the second half of the year. From those team meetings, it was clear that Bujar was a natural leader. He was extremely organized in leading group projects, and considerate in assigning roles to teammates. A lifelong humanitarian, he later agreed to join the GPBF Advisory Board and, ultimately, its board of directors.

Bujar can trace his decision to become a humanitarian nearly all the way back to childhood. In April 1999, he became a refugee at age nineteen, fleeing Kosovo with his family to escape persecution and the war with Serbia. They were caught by Serbian police days later, however, and Bujar feared his family would be assassinated. By what he attributes to luck alone, Bujar and his family were forced onto an overcrowded train headed for Macedonia. As the train pulled away, he recalls feeling his life's progress and efforts disappearing with it. He had no photos of family or his life back at home and very few belongings, and was daunted by the thought of starting over.

When he was processed into the Stankovic refugee camp, he felt his life languishing in the muddy, overcrowded camp. He saw his options as feeling hopeless and waiting for help, or volunteering and supporting fellow refugees. Bujar chose the latter, and felt my youth. Perhaps the genocide in Rwanda could have been predicted, and measures taken to mitigate the killing.

A few years later, a peace building colleague, Milt Lauenstein, referred me to a book entitled *Peaceland*, written by Severine Autesserre. The author provides a good explanation of what gives rise to "not having a clue" regarding an impending mass atrocity:

> The expatriates' deficient understanding of local contexts prompts them to employ ready-to-use templates of conflict resolution, even when these universal models are ill-suited to local conditions. The routine absence of close relationships between interveners and their local counterparts reinforces the foreigners' tendency to create parallel systems of governance. Their frequent disregard of local knowledge legitimizes their rapid turnover from country to country, as acquiring thematic experience in a variety of conflict settings takes precedent over developing an in-depth understanding of a specific situation. Moreover, their lack of local knowledge enables many of the peacebuilders to view as acceptable short-term and top-down approaches to complex political, economic, and social problems.

The presentation by the U.S. foreign service officer, coupled with further research

connected with the cause. He valued the ability to provide hope to people. His efforts led to the opening of the first school within the camp, and the hope he saw in students' eyes gave him hope.

This choice to support his fellow refugees evolved into a real passion for vulnerable communities, and eventually became Bujar's global career and mission. He has since worked with some of the world's most upstanding organizations, including CARE International, Save the Children, and USAID. He's worked with countless communities in countries such as Lebanon, Syria, Jordan, Turkey, Egypt, Iraq, Macedonia, Albania, and his beloved Kosovo. His response to his seriously traumatic childhood experience was not to follow the example of human violence, but to combat it.

Bujar's work since then has centered on saving lives in emergencies and conflict-affected zones, creating safe environments for the most vulnerable in different communities to rebuild their future, and promoting social justice and peace for those affected by discrimination. His refugee experience led to a deep affinity and connection with people who are suffering as a result of conflict, displacement, or socio-economic inequity.

—

and reading, turned out to be one of my most significant takeaways from my GMAP time in Lisbon. I learned the importance of locally led peace building efforts at the grassroots level.

At night, many of us found time to stroll through the streets of Lisbon, hang out at some of its many small bars and restaurants, and engage in lively discussions about global affairs and the state of the world. I recruited a few of my classmates to join me one evening at a fado house. (Fado, like the blues, is an expression of longing and sorrow, and is the music of Lisbon.) There was never a dull moment during my time there. I regularly returned to my hotel room around 11:00 p.m., just in time to hit the sack, get a good night's rest, and start all over again at the crack of dawn. I was energized, and I cherished the time there. In a way, it was an escape from reality, and I didn't want it to end.

The GMAP staff did a great job in organizing a field trip for Saturday, January 9. The weather was cool and sunny as we boarded a bus at our hotel that morning shortly after breakfast. We departed from Lisbon, headed northwest, and traveled along the rocky Atlantic coast. We passed the resort town of Cascais on the way to Sintra, a beautiful hill town dotted with historic palaces surrounded by wooded hills, a favorite summer retreat for the kings of Portugal. (The town was recognized as a UNESCO World Heritage site in 1995.) We visited two of the palaces and stopped for a casual, lengthy lunch at a restaurant perched atop a mountain. It was a splendid afternoon and a welcome respite from the academic routine of the week before.

On our way back to Lisbon, we stopped along the coastline at a place called Cabo da Roca, the westernmost point of the European continent. It is a significant and inspiring place, with a lighthouse dating back to 1772 overlooking the vast Atlantic Ocean; it's also among the eight hundred geographical points throughout the world that have been dedicated to peace through the Sri Chinmoy Peace Blossoms program. We returned from our field trip just in time for our Saturday night dinner at the hotel.

One entire day the following week was dedicated to a Crisis Simulation Exercise for our Security Studies and Crisis Management class. My team was assigned to role-play as the United States in the crisis simulation, and my teammates asked me to be the President, which is what they had called me since the beginning of the residency. My main takeaway from the simulation exercise was how easily a crisis can get out of control when conflict erupts, even when you're a major player like the U.S. Even though the U.S. was big and powerful, we were inept and slow to react to the smaller, faster, and more efficient non-state actors, commonly referred to as terrorist organizations. I imagined I knew what it must have been like for Bush and Cheney on September 11, 2001, and the days, weeks, and months that followed, and I felt myself gaining empathy for them.

The two-week Lisbon residency quickly came to an end. I was physically weary, but emotionally strong and confident as I headed home. I was ready to take on the next phase of the remote learning— and I was no longer afraid. I knew how the process worked: extensive reading and writing; listening to lectures via video; posting on the boards; team projects; and weekly team meetings via Skype. I was eager to delve into the thesis proposal and research; my heart was in writing my thesis and finding my path.

I realized that my time was going to be stretched to the limits: I was headed into the busy tax season in my CPA practice, and it was going to be a real juggling act. But I was not afraid to take it all on; I felt emboldened. The feeling reminded me of when I led my eighth-grade basketball team out of the locker room onto the court amid loud cheering from the spectators in the St. Anne School gymnasium.

The pent-up excitement within me had exploded the second I stepped onto the court and sprinted down towards the hoop. I experienced that same feeling as the plane lifted from the tarmac in Lisbon and we ascended into the air; I felt the excitement once again explode and the adrenaline kick in.

———

CHAPTER SIXTEEN
Blueprint for a Thesis

Our GMAP thesis project was kickstarted in Lisbon. Dean Nutter had told us on January 3 that each of us would meet with Nicholas (Nick) Kenney in Lisbon to begin preparing our thesis proposal. She'd also talked briefly about the structure: first a hypothesis (a statement that answers the research question), then a methodology (the type of method you'll use to test your hypothesis). She mentioned that most GMAPers use a case-study method. Finally, she recommended that we review the book *Craft of Research*, which had been given to us during the August residency in Boston, and told us to pay particular attention to its citation guidelines.

I had never written a thesis and was intimidated by the thought. But the Fletcher School again allayed my fears. I soon realized in Lisbon that the GMAP staff, particularly Nick Kenney, would provide the structure and the resources to make my thesis a success. All I had to do was follow the structure and do the work. Moreover, after I read Nick Kenney's biography, I felt that he was well suited to help me with my thesis—his background was perfect for my thesis topic.

Nick, a doctoral candidate at the Fletcher School, earned his Master of Arts in Law and Diplomacy from the Fletcher School in 2008, and wrote his master's thesis on Northern Ireland's Good Friday peace process, a topic of great interest to me. His fields of study in the Fletcher School's doctoral program included international negotiation and conflict resolution. In 2007, he worked in Jerusalem for a conflict resolution NGO, Search for Common Ground, later to become the subject of one of my thesis case studies. He also held a J.D. from Boston College Law School, where he concentrated in international law, and studied abroad at the London School of Economics and King's College, with a B.A. in history from the College of Holy Cross. He'd been valedictorian of his class. When I first sat down with Nick in Lisbon, I thought he was way too young to have already accomplished all of this.

Nick was in Lisbon during the entire residency, available to meet with us and help us along the way. I felt very fortunate at the beginning of the Lisbon residency that I already knew what I wanted to write about: peace building activities at the grassroots level by ordinary citizens, known in the academic world as Track Three peace building.

On January 5, Nick and I met at a small table in a dimly lit hallway of the hotel, for our first step in the process of developing the one-page proposal.

Nick handed me the four-page GMAP Writing Materials Guide that he and another doctoral student, Emma Belcher, had written. (I would meet Emma four years later in the peace building world.) I really liked that we were getting started with the basics. As I read the guide, my mind drifted for a moment as I recalled the story about the famous UCLA basketball coach, John Wooden, who had taken time at the beginning of each season's first practice to teach his team how to put their shoes and socks on, and how to properly tie the shoes. It sounds silly, but it's true: very basic—but very important. And that little exercise paid dividends—it kept players from getting blisters from the quick starts and stops inherent in competitive basketball. In my mind, GMAP was doing the right thing. So simple, but so important.

Nick then handed me a one-page document that outlined the format of the thesis proposal, to be approved before I could submit it to my thesis advisor, Professor Chigas. This document would serve as the foundation of my thesis:

Topic: *In 10 words or less—what is your thesis about?*

Context: *The background of your thesis, why it is important*

Research Question: *A clear question you will answer in your thesis*

Hypothesis: *Your hypothesized answer to your research question*

Methodology: *Case studies, qualitative analysis, statistical analysis, comparative analysis, etc.*

Seems simple, right? But it turned out to be an arduous undertaking.

In my meeting with Nick, I felt challenged by his initial questions. He told me that, compared to Tracks One and Two, Track Three diplomacy was a new term, with limited literature. He asked me who coined the term, and I told him that I didn't know, but would research it and find the answer. He requested that I include a definition of Track Three diplomacy in my thesis proposal, then fired off a series of questions: "Is Track Three effective? How do we know that we're making an impact? Does it reduce conflict?" Uncertain, I shrugged my shoulders. Nick warned me, "Skeptics will say that this work is being done by a bunch of do-gooder NGOs. Is this perception accurate? Do the NGOs have realistic ambitions, or are they purely idealistic?" I grimaced.

A key question, he remarked, was, *What is the impact, and how do you measure it?* He concluded by telling me that my case studies would require engaged research to answer the question, *Who has done it well, and why?*

After our meeting, I realized I had to dig deeper and learn much more about Track Three diplomacy. I was impressed with Nick's humility and kindness; he was respectful and took a collaborative approach, readily admitting that he didn't know much about Track

Three diplomacy. He didn't have all the answers, but he certainly asked the right questions.

I submitted my initial thesis proposal to Nick on January 12, a week after our initial meeting, while I was still in Lisbon. I received his feedback on January 22, after I returned home to Pittsburgh. He told me that I still needed to find a definition of Track Three diplomacy and align my case studies to the definition. On February 10, I submitted a second proposal to Nick. (**See Appendix A.**) This one was approved, and I received Nick's approval to send it to Professor Chigas and proceed with my research—though he noted that I needed to delve more into case study selection.

I had read Professor Chigas's biography before the very first lecture of our International Negotiation class, during the first residency in Boston in August 2009. I hoped that I would be able to get to know her better, and that perhaps she might be able to help me in my search for a peace and justice ministry. The second I first spoke to her, I sensed that yet another angel had been placed in my midst.

I had approached Professor Chigas during our very first coffee break on the first day at the Fletcher School. When I said

Diana Chigas

Diana Chigas did not set out with the goal of becoming an international negotiation expert and educator. After she graduated from Yale with a degree in French Literature in 1979, she became a paralegal and worked with a divorce law firm.

"I saw a lot of people being really awful to each other," she says. "In the back of my mind, I kept thinking, *There has to be a better way.*"

Thirty years later, Diana is now one of the foremost thought leaders in building those better ways. Her work has taken her to the locations of some of the most intractable conflicts around the world, including El Salvador, South Africa, Ecuador, Peru, Georgia, and Cyprus. She has facilitated training sessions for some of the largest international organizations, like the United Nations and the Organization for Security and Cooperation in Europe.

After working as a paralegal, Diana attended Harvard Law School. As she approached graduation, she was considering practicing international law in London, but her father became ill and she decided not to go. Instead, she joined Conflict Management Group (CMG), founded by one of her professors, Roger Fisher.

Diana's first assignment was in South Africa, and she went on to work with CMG for sixteen years, flung into one conflict after another with the near-impossible task of finding durable solutions.

"I kept going because I saw a lot of personal transformations," she says now, with as much enthusiasm as if it were yesterday. "At some level, you could say this was simple stuff, but it was really powerful to people when hello and I introduced myself, I sensed that somehow she already knew me. She was welcoming, warm, and friendly. Her humility came through when she asked me, "How am I doing?"—in essence, asking me if her lecture had been acceptable! I liked her from the very beginning. Her personality reinforced my long-held belief that the great ones are always humble. I was truly blessed to have her on my journey; she turned out to be a real treasure.

Professor Chigas brought so much to the table. She had a distinguished academic background: a J.D. from Harvard Law School; a Master of Arts in Law and Diplomacy from the Fletcher School; and a B.A. from Yale. In addition, she was engaged as a practitioner as Co-director of Collaborative Learning at CDA, based in Cambridge, Massachusetts. She had several years of experience as a facilitator and consultant in negotiation and conflict resolution settings. Moreover, she had written extensively in the peace building field.

On February 10, I emailed my thesis proposal to Professor Chigas, along with questions for her about readings and additional case studies. She and I spoke later in March, and she sent me a substantial follow-up email on March 28 that included

they could figure out ways of connecting across the differences.

"It was fulfilling. After ten years, I started thinking, *We're doing a lot of work...but is it adding up?* A lot of colleagues who had now become personal friends were still struggling and getting lots of pushback. People were still marginalized. I started questioning how I could move this to a bigger impact space."

She shifted to CDA Collaborative Learning Projects, a non-governmental organization dedicated to working with development, humanitarian, and peace building practitioners and the private sector globally to improve the effectiveness of international assistance in fragile and conflict-affected contexts.

"I had another *a-ha* moment while reflecting at CDA," she says. "I started to think about systems, partly out of thinking about how to scale up our work. I found we made a lot of assumptions about what our work results would be, without testing them first. My time at CDA allowed me to take a step back and realize there's not a linear path from here to there."

This reflection, in addition to her time working in Cyprus, would affect how Diana looked at conflict resolution. "There was a time before the 2004 referendum when we were doing a high-level Track Two peace process," she recalls. "It was the first time after ten years there that I thought, *They can really engage with each other in a very different way than before.* Change takes a very long time."

Corruption is Diana's latest focus area. She started teaching part-time at the Fletcher School in the early 2000s, covering a class for a colleague who was on sabbatical, which enabled her to dig suggested research paths and initial reading recommendations. It was apparent that she put a lot of thought into that email, and I really appreciated her thoughtfulness.

She recommended eight books that provided me with a strong base of general knowledge about Track Three. **(These books are included in the Thesis Bibliography in Appendix B.)**

My major takeaways from these books were:

Lasting peace can and must be built from the bottom up by ordinary citizens.

Power resides not just with high-level decision-makers, but at the grassroots level as well.

Each individual can make a difference.

Diplomacy is fundamentally about relationships.

Sustainable peace is rooted in relationships that maintain a sense of connectedness, trust, respect, and the ability to communicate in a non-violent manner. These elements of relationships are essential to building and maintaining long-term sustainable peace.

These takeaways struck a chord with me, as they aligned with my personal beliefs.

In that same email, Professor Chigas also recommended that I learn more about something called Contact Theory, and listed

into issues around corruption and social norms and the intersection of peace building and corruption.

"For me, teaching provided an opportunity to keep up to speed on literature and the latest research that was relevant to my own work," she says. "I could bring some of what I was thinking through in teaching back to my work—it enabled me to blend theory and practice. Fletcher is a great place," she adds. "I wouldn't have gone anywhere to teach, but as an alum of Fletcher, I knew that students came from places of blending theory and practice."

At Fletcher, Diana now also serves as the Senior International Officer and Associate Provost and co-directs the Corruption, Justice, and Legitimacy (CJL) program at Fletcher's Leir Institute, a research-to-practice initiative created to improve the effectiveness of anti-corruption programming in fragile and conflict-affected contexts.

several relevant publications. She wrote, "These are important theoretical background for anything you might want to look at that has inter-group contact as a basis for breaking down stereotypes, enemy images, etc."

Professor Chigas followed up with yet another substantial email that homed in on Contact Theory. That email contained an additional reading list of over a dozen books and articles. **(See Appendix B.)**

At the time, amid time pressures and looming deadlines, I didn't realize the full significance of those two emails in March and June from Professor Chigas. The reading lists that she'd shared with me would profoundly influence how I built my thesis, by introducing me to the idea that "changing attitudes and relationships is important to peace building, and doing this at the grassroots level will contribute to peace." This, in turn, would profoundly change my life and propel me toward connecting the world at large, at the grassroots level, through relationships based on mutual trust and respect—the bedrock of peace.

Contact Theory

The Contact Theory, developed in the 1950s by Gordon Allport, PhD, is a theory of change based on the concept that a lack of contact and unfamiliarity between conflicting groups can and often does breed attitudes such as stereotyping and prejudice which can potentially escalate into hostility and violence. The theory believes that these negative attitudes can be reduced by promoting contact and familiarity between conflicting groups.

A 2001 study by Thomas Pettigrew, PhD, finds that all that is needed for greater understanding between groups is contact, period, in all but hostile and threatening conditions. The reason contact works, his analysis finds, is not purely or even mostly cognitive, but emotional. Pettigrew explains, "Your stereotypes about the other group don't necessary change, but you grow to like them anyway."

CHAPTER SEVENTEEN

Water Trickles Through

I chose to use real-life case studies as my methodology to illustrate how the Contact Theory works in the real world—in essence, merging practice with theory. In April, I began to search more actively for Track Three organizations; more specifically, I looked for organizations engaged in grassroots diplomacy, as defined by Louise Diamond and John McDonald in their book, *Multi-Track Diplomacy: A Systems Approach to Peace*:

"Grassroots diplomacy seeks to establish personal relationships with people from other nations and cultures and, through those relationships, to address issues of mutual concern, break down stereotypes and promote friendship, provide needed resources, and educate the public and the policymakers on international peace and development issues."

I learned that this kind of diplomacy is characterized by long-term relationship building and transformational activities.

My search for organizations operating at the grassroots level was not clear-cut. I knew I just had to follow, trust in, and be led by the spirit. My original thesis proposal, submitted and approved on February 10, listed three proposed case-study subjects: The American Ireland Fund, The Foundation for West Africa, and Seeds of Peace (SOP).

I found SOP via a traditional academic pursuit—in my early readings. I contacted Leslie Lewin, the organization's executive director, who was located in New York City. She was quite friendly and referred me to Eva Gordan, SOP's Director of Strategic Initiatives, more conveniently located in Boston. Eva and I had several telephone and email exchanges, and we were able to meet in person for lunch as I neared completion of my thesis. Eva was most generous with her time, and she was a great resource for me. Finding SOP and developing the case study, largely with Eva's help, turned out to be a walk in the park.

Though I didn't end up including either of them directly, both the American Ireland Fund and the Foundation for West Africa inadvertently led me to the other two case studies I did include in my thesis. It was a somewhat random path of discovery.

———

Kathleen Rooney had first told me about the American Ireland Fund (AIF) way back in the mid-1970s when she and I were college students. She was excited to let me know that her dad, Dan Rooney, and Tony O'Reilly, then CEO of the Heinz Corporation, had started the fund to support programs of peace and reconciliation, arts and culture, community development, and education in Ireland. After Kathleen's death I didn't follow the activities of the AIF until 2005, when Tom Miller invited me to join him at the organization's annual fundraiser event in Pittsburgh. I was amazed at how much the AIF had grown since its inception; at the date of my thesis research and writing, the organization had raised more than $300 million.

The Fletcher School gave us a brief break in mid-April, so Phyllis and I took advantage of the time off and flew to New York City for a getaway. My GMAP teammate Ruth Lande was gracious enough to let us stay in a guest apartment in the apartment building she and her husband John owned.

While in New York, Phyllis and I met with Caitlin McCormick

and Kieran McLoughlin of the AIF. Professor Chigas had told me that she'd heard of the AIF, and commented that she didn't see how the AIF would be a good fit for my thesis—it wasn't really operating at the grassroots level, but rather, raising money and supporting grassroots organizations in Ireland—but it seemed like a good place to start in finding other such organizations. Our meeting with Caitlin and Kieran lasted ten minutes at most; we discussed my thesis project and I asked them to help me connect with some of the NGOs in Ireland that were doing peace building work on the ground. Within a week or so, Caitlin had emailed me a list of grassroots peace building organizations.

Peace Players International (PPI), a successful integration program incorporating basketball, caught my eye. Trevor Ringland, located in Belfast, was listed as the contact person. Trevor turned out to be a great resource, and PPI an excellent fit for my thesis. (It would also later become one of the GPBF's longstanding grantees.)

It was worth taking the time to travel to New York and have that brief meeting with Caitlin and Kieran. And I felt Kathleen's presence for a moment as the bright sunshine streamed through the window of Kieran's tiny little office in Manhattan. She was with us in spirit.

I read about the Foundation for West Africa (FWA) on the Fletcher School's website. The website mentioned that the International Negotiation and Conflict Resolution Club at the Fletcher School hosted the FWA to speak about the utility of radio as a mechanism for peace, accountability, and stability in West Africa. The FWA targeted West Africa's core needs: accountable governance, human rights, healthcare, and sustainable economic development.

I contacted Topher Hamblett, the founder and president of the

FWA. Topher told me that the organization, headquartered in Rhode Island, was a donor of the NGO doing the work on the ground in West Africa, Search for Common Ground (SFCG). He suggested that I contact Rebecca Besant, the program manager for the Africa program. Rebecca was an excellent resource, and SFCG became the third and final case study in my thesis.

I had several communications with Topher, via telephone and email, during and even after the development of the SFCG case study. The FWA's business model struck a chord with me—it was a small public foundation, issuing micro-grants to NGOs to support their peace building work on the ground, resulting in outsized impact. (I would adopt this same business model when I created my own foundation.) This was a bonus finding that the case-study approach made possible.

By using the case-study methodology for my thesis, I was able to focus on three different grassroots peace building approaches in three different regions of the world: SOP, which used dialogue programs with youth from Middle Eastern countries; SFCG, which used media in West Africa: and PPI, which used an integration program built around basketball in Northern Ireland.

Contributions to the Peace Process

Here are the questions I posed to Eva Gordon (SOP), Rebecca Besant (SFCG), Trevor Ringland (PPI), Topher Hamblett (FWA), and Caitriona Fottrell (Ireland Funds) about how their work affects the peace process, along with their responses.

Eva Gordon (SOP)

Q: How do you see the work that is done through Seeds of Peace contributing, or having an effect or impact on, the overall peace process in the Middle East—the Israeli and Palestinian conflict?

A: The answer is somewhat simple. [SOP founder] John Wallach always said, "Governments sign treaties, but only people can make peace." Regardless of how many peace agreements/treaties are signed, it will only become a reality through people's willingness and ability to live together and coexist. Seeds of Peace, therefore, helps to create the conditions necessary for peace to take root by enabling people to form relationships across borders based on empathy, trust, and an appreciation for the narratives/perspectives/needs of "the other side."

Rebecca Besant (SFCG)

Q: How do you see the work that is done through SFCG contributing, or having an effect or impact on, the overall peace process in Sierra Leone?

A: I think in the time immediately following the peace process and during the transition period, it was about bringing different voices into the process, breaking down stereotypes and misperceptions that people had about each other, and making sure that everyone understood different steps of

The case studies illustrated how, through dialogue, integration, and media, stereotyping, prejudices, hatreds, and fears are broken down and individual relationships are transformed. This reinforced what I had learned from my readings. Moreover, I began to experience a vision of the real possibility of how the impact of these individual transformations can have a ripple effect on peace in the world, as these experiences are transferred to others.

I learned in my readings, however, that there was a great deal of pushback to the notion that changing attitudes and relationships at the grassroots level could contribute to peace in the world. It was disappointing to me to read the negative opinions expressed by the critics, whose major challenge was, "How do you measure the impact?" It's true that we live in a world that is data-driven, where results must be tangible and quantifiable—but admittedly, the results of these efforts are qualitative in nature.

Fortunately, I learned that there were legitimate attempts being made by peace building organizations to measure or quantify their impact, and this would not prove to be a deterrent for me in proceeding with the creation of the GPBF. This was largely due to the inspiration I received from my

the process (repatriation, disarmament, etc.) and how they would or would not benefit. New and different space was created where people could talk about issues and try to find collaborative ways to solve them. We could help bring these different groups into these discussions where they wouldn't be able to bring themselves there because of power dynamics, perceptions, etc. As this went along, it created new social models for participation and acceptance. So women could talk on the radio and not be scorned by the community, or youth could have an association and advocate for their rights, or people could ask questions of their leaders and expect an answer.

Topher Hamblett (FWA)
Q: How do you see the work that is done through SFCG contributing, or having an effect or impact on, the overall peace process in Sierra Leone?
A: The work that FWA does through SFCG is making a major contribution to peace in Sierra Leone. We are providing some of the hardware (equipment) that is essential to large-scale promotion of peaceful conduct during elections. This is accomplished by direct messaging that encourages peaceful conduct, but also by educating voters about the process and their rights as citizens. And by broadcasting polling results in real time or near real time, radio stations are creating an environment where rumors can be snuffed out and real, accurate information is shared by all. Violence can occur in conditions of uncertainty, so we are helping with the flow of information—in local languages—throughout the country. Beyond elections, FWA's support of SFCG is helping to create an environment where conflicts are resolved

interviews with the people doing the work on the ground, as I dug deeper into my three case studies.

———

I discovered, through the SOP case study, the power of dialogue in peace building processes. I gained insight into this via my experience of the SOP dialogue sessions, which were supervised by trained facilitators and held over a three-week period at SOP's international peace camp in Otisfield, Maine.

Early on, the participants (mostly Israeli, Palestinian, and Egyptian youth) begin to see the human faces of those they were raised to hate, and from that experience build relationships around mutual trust and respect. A transformation then takes place. In week one, the participants express anger, pain, and suffering. In week two, they begin listening to other perspectives. In week three, they start to discuss how they can put the past behind them, move forward, and explore ways to live in safety and peace.

Year-round regional programming in the home countries provides a support system when the participants return home to conflict zones, and graduates of the program, referred to as Seeds, become leaders and advocates for peace in their home communities through

more openly and peacefully. SFCG and community radio stations are frequently asked by community members to come in and resolve conflicts that can easily escalate into violence. They are considered trusted mediators, and we are pleased to support their work. Also, it is important that the young people of Sierra Leone be exposed to peaceful ways of resolving conflict. So this is a long-term investment in peace.

Trevor Ringland (PPI)

Q: How do you see the work that is done through PPI contributing, or having an effect or impact on, the overall peace process in Northern Ireland?"

A: At its simplest it gives children a chance to meet and build relationships they would not otherwise get a chance to make. However, it importantly shows a different way if society gives the necessary leadership, and that there is an appetite for that in parents and teachers. It is a great example that if you make friends, you destroy enemies. Also, with PPI's special skills and expertise we can be the icebreakers in difficult areas, with others taking over and building on the opportunity created.

Caitriona Fottrell (Ireland Funds, a donor of PPI in Northern Ireland)

Q: How do you see the work that is done through PPI contributing, or having an effect or impact on, the overall peace process in Northern Ireland?

A: It is too early to tell the long-term effect of the program. It is an attractive program, fun, dynamic and worthwhile. It is a way to get the adults and teachers involved as well. It is well run. PeacePlayers takes a strategic approach: they go into areas community-service projects, educational programs, and even starting their own peace building NGOs. Through these endeavors, Seeds provide a fine example of the ripple effect.

The SFCG case study showed me how media—e.g., radio and television programming—helps prevent and transform conflict by challenging stereotypes, providing reliable and balanced information, and promoting dialogue and reconciliation. These activities are aligned with SFCG's fundamental goal to "understand the differences and act on the commonalities."

I was impressed that SFCG developed media models that involved putting children and women on the radio, providing them with an opportunity to have a voice. A children's news program was developed, for example, that was partially reported and produced by children. The program gave the children a forum to discuss their hopes and fears and advocate for issues important to them.

And what a difference SFCG and FWA were making in Sierra Leone! This was not a quick fix, but rather a long-term process, conducted at the local community level, to benefit future generations. And in Burundi, SFCG implemented joint reporting teams

where there is zero integration...it is a big challenge in the working-class areas. It is reaching out to the marginalized areas. The American involvement is an attractive feature as well.

(Hutus and Tutsis) in media projects focused on ethnicity issues. I couldn't help but think of the stark contrast to how media was used as an evil tool to perpetrate genocide between the Hutus and Tutsis in Rwanda.

I was in for a similar revelation with the PPI case study, which illustrated to me how sports can be used to unite and educate young people in divided communities.

PPI operates on the premise that "children who play together can learn to live together." In Northern Ireland, basketball is used to integrate Catholic and Protestant children, aged ten to fourteen, to play together on mixed teams. The teamwork builds mutual respect and friendships. According to Trevor Ringland, the program is at the early stage or front end of breaking down barriers—"doing stuff at the 'hard edge,' with the children at an early age, with the hope that as the children grow older, they continue to develop and be influenced in a positive way with other community programs."

According to Ringland, the youth's participation in PPI is an example of the impact of one small step. "This is how leadership is shown," he says. "Barriers are broken down, teachers and parents become involved, and it then has a wider impact on the local community … that is the impact of the program, and it can't be measured. It's the right thing to do—influencing children and those around them with the hope that the children will influence their peer groups."

CHAPTER EIGHTEEN
Down the Homestretch

As I completed my studies and thesis at the Fletcher School, I experienced yet another opening—a whole new world was opened to me. It was evident to me that the people I met in my thesis research were passionate about and committed to their work. Their organizations were providing alternative solutions to violent conflict for the world. They were providing an antidote to hatred, fear, and violent dehumanizing behavior towards the "scary other" by teaching youth and children how to get to know each other as human beings, across ethnic, cultural, and religious differences. They were seeking to undo the hatred, fear, and violence that had been passed from one generation to the next. And I soon realized how I could help them.

I could create a charitable organization, a public foundation, like Topher Hamblett's FWA. (A public foundation uses publicly collected funds to directly support its initiatives.) My vision was not to limit my foundation's support to a specific geographic region. Rather, the foundation I envisioned would be global in scope—it would create awareness all over the world and raise money to support global grassroots peace building efforts. I could see how such a foundation would support grantee programs and projects in dialogue, sports, and the arts all over the world.

I believed that this approach would be simple and cost-effective. I could see how $500 to $1,000 microgrants would go a long way and make an outsized impact. I believed that this approach would be more effective in preventing future mass atrocities (such as Rwanda) and terrorist attacks (such as another 9/11). It would be a proactive, not a reactive, approach.

Just six weeks after I completed my studies at the Fletcher School, with the date of incorporation on September 11, 2010, the tax-exempt, nonprofit corporation called the Foundation for Global Peace Building was established. We subsequently changed the name to the Global Peace Building Foundation, or GPBF.

―――

Even though I'd completed all my course work, received a passing grade for my thesis, and passed the final exams, I still had one more major requirement to fulfill before I would get my Fletcher degree—a passing grade on a foreign-language reading comprehension and conversation exam. I chose Spanish, because I had studied Spanish in high school and college. I tried, initially, to prepare for these exams during the academic year while I completed all the other degree requirements. I signed up for an adult-education Spanish class one evening a week at the Mount Lebanon High School, taught by Eugenia Chirino, and I attended the first three or four classes but ran out of steam. It was just too much for me to take on learning Spanish in addition to my other Fletcher courses and the time demands of my CPA practice, not to mention family life.

The Fletcher School gave me until one year after graduation, July 24, 2011, to complete the foreign-language competency exams. The clock was ticking; the pressure was on. All the previous year's academic work would have been for naught if I didn't pass the Spanish exams, and I knew that the Fletcher degree would provide me with much-needed credibility in the global peace building field.

Fortunately, the GMAP staff was once again there to support me. I received a simple but great piece of advice from Endri Misho, a member of the GMAP administrative team, on the morning before our graduation ceremony. The GMAP staff had arranged for a bus to transport my classmates and me to Henrietta's Table, a restaurant located in Harvard Square, in Cambridge, where we were treated to a voluptuous brunch. It was another of the first-class social gatherings that I'd become accustomed to at the Fletcher School. We were all pretty much exhausted at that point, so it was time for us to kick back, relax, and enjoy a good meal together. There were several toasts given in a spirit of thanks and gratitude—after all, we were just a day away from graduation, and all our hardest work was now behind us—but I knew that I had a little more work cut out for me.

Endri sat down next to me at one of the big round tables, and brought up the topic of my impending foreign-language exams. "Tom," he said, "I recommend that you take a month off after graduation and relax before you begin preparing for the Spanish exams." Surprised, I thanked him. If it had not been for that piece of advice, I would have jumped right in without giving my brain a much-needed respite. Taking a month off, as it turned out, was exactly the right thing to do.

———

I was riding my bicycle on my favorite bike trail on a bright, hot, and humid Saturday morning in August when I had to slow down and come to an abrupt stop. A woman and her daughter, also on bikes, were slowly entering the trail at the juncture. I was worried that I was going to collide with them, because they weren't paying attention to their surroundings—they appeared to be inexperienced riders. As I cautiously passed them, I realized the mother looked familiar—it was Eugenia, my Spanish teacher at the Mt. Lebanon adult-education program. Right away, she recognized me too and called out, "Tom!"

It was a serendipitous moment—the first and only time I ever saw Eugenia on the bike trail. I pulled over to the side of the trail, and she and I talked for a few minutes. I apologized for quitting her Spanish class, and she told me she wasn't surprised. She said I'd looked very tired during the few classes that I'd attended. I asked her if she would be willing to be my tutor and help me prepare for my Spanish reading comprehension and conversation exams. She told me that she would help me—and another angel entered my life.

Eugenia was a true blessing. She'd grown up in Mexico City and now lived in Peters Township, within a short drive from Mt. Lebanon. Spanish was her native language, and she spoke excellent English as well. She was raising two young daughters, but she made time for me. She recommended that I buy a Spanish textbook, and she assigned readings for me to complete and review with her in subsequent classes. She and I met every Friday morning, starting in September, at a local library, and practiced speaking Spanish during our sessions, which lasted until I passed my exams.

My daughter Katie, a teacher by profession, took the initiative and prepared index cards for me with an assortment of Spanish prepositions, verbs, adverbs, nouns, adjectives, idioms, and expressions. In all, there were about a hundred cards to help me memorize these commonly used words and expressions. It really helped me read, and hear, the language.

I also bought a software package to help me practice speaking and hearing Spanish on my desktop computer. Eugenia recommended that I watch Spanish television programs, especially soap operas, to help me process the language, so I did that on a regular basis in the evenings, and watched a morning news program telecast from Chile.

I pulled out all the stops ... and this wide assortment of preparation paid off. I passed the reading comprehension exam on my third attempt. I took the exam at Duquesne University, where Duquesne and Tufts arranged a proctor so I wouldn't have to travel to Boston. I anxiously watched the clock tick away while I completed the reading and translation, and finished the exam just in the nick of time. I had just finished my final paragraph and looked up at the clock, and within a few minutes the proctor walked in and told me my time was up. The spirit was with me in that room that morning! Endri telephoned me when he got word that I'd passed the written exam, and continued to cheer me on.

I took the oral examination on the afternoon of Friday, June 17—with my deadline being July 24. The Fletcher School allowed me to take the oral exam via telephone with the language professor in Boston, so Eugenia and I prepared for the oral exam by having several telephone conversations leading up to the exam date. I was more nervous about taking the oral examination than about presenting my thesis to Professor Chigas! There was so much on the line, and I was running out of time. I felt so much pressure.

I called the professor in the afternoon of June 17, as scheduled. She answered the phone speaking Spanish, and we spoke Spanish until the very end of the conversation, when she said to me, in English, "Tom, congratulations—you passed!"

I said to her, in Spanish, "I want to give you a big hug!" We both laughed.

I was so relieved—it had been one of the most stressful experiences in my life. You'd think that it would be a time for celebration that evening. Instead, I went to bed early. I was emotionally drained.

The Master of Arts degree in International Relations from the Fletcher School of Law and Diplomacy was issued to me on August 31, 2011. Enclosed in a Fletcher School frame and prominently displayed in my office, this coveted degree serves as a daily reminder for me of a dream come true, and of the work that lies ahead.

—

PART 3

It's a philosophy of life. A practice.
If you do this, something will change, what will change is
that you will change,
your life will change, and if you can change you,
you can perhaps change the world.

—VIVIENNE WESTWOOD

CHAPTER NINETEEN
Launching the GPBF

The time 9:11 continued to appear to me at unexpected times, even though I wasn't purposely looking for it. I'm not one to be focused on the time; I don't even wear a watch.

In one instance, while I was traveling overnight, I returned to my hotel room and stopped at the door to check the time on my cell phone. I was debating on whether to call Phyllis, thinking that it may be too late to call. The time on my cell phone was 9:18 when I opened the door. When I walked into my room, I noticed the time on the clock on the nightstand next to the bed: 9:11.

One morning, as I sat down at my desk, I noticed that I hadn't turned off my timer (which I use to track my time) the night before. The time on the timer was 9:11—nine hours and eleven minutes. I took a picture of it to memorialize what I considered a message from above.

Recognizing these occurrences as divine intervention, via Angel Katie, continued to remind me that my purpose at this stage of my life is to contribute to building peace and making the world a better place. I felt a strong force calling me to stay with this purpose, work through the obstacles, and get the GBPF off the ground.

Our first Board of Directors meeting was held at the Allegheny HYP Club in Pittsburgh on October 26, 2010. Phyllis attended this inaugural meeting in an unofficial capacity, to show her support. William

E. Markus, my college professor, mentor, and friend, and a lecturer of international relations, joined me to start the new venture. Carole O. Markus, his wife, also enthusiastically agreed to join us. She brought a keen knowledge of non-profit organization governance to the table. Bill and Carole would go on to serve on our board of directors for the first four years. With their enthusiasm, commitment, knowledge, and wisdom, we got off to the right start.

In our first meeting, I recommended that we develop a theme or focus and narrow the scope of our grantmaking specifically to peace building related to children and youth. I had always been saddened by the fact that children subjected to violent conflict have no voice, and I had been inspired by my thesis case-study research, particularly by how peace building work can transform young people's lives. I believed that the GPBF, through its grantmaking, could undo the hatred, fear, and violence that passes from one generation to the next; our work would break the cycle, and by doing so, contribute to the building of sustainable peace that all children deserve.

Bill suggested that children and youth need a curriculum to learn how to minimize conflict and to reinforce non-violent behavior. Carole recommended that the "butterfly prin-

William E. Markus

I first met Professor William Markus in the fall of 1975 during my second year of undergraduate studies at Duquesne University, when I took his class on International Relations. As I look back on my life, I realize that in him, I was blessed with another angel who entered and became part of my life.

Bill Markus fascinated me. I took every class that he taught at Duquesne, and regularly visited him during his office hours in the afternoon. I really enjoyed being with Bill during those afternoon meetings as we discussed global affairs; I learned so much from him. He and his wife Carole had traveled all over the world, and generously shared his experiences with me. He had graduated from Harvard, and mentioned that two of his Harvard professors had gone on to serve in U.S. presidential administrations: McGeorge Bundy had served as U.S. National Security Advisor to Presidents John F. Kennedy and Lyndon Johnson; and Zbigniew Brzezinski had served as Counselor to President Johnson and then National Security Advisor to President Jimmy Carter. This impressed me, and I often thought about what it would be like to be a student at a prestigious institution like Harvard and sit in on lectures presented by leading practitioners in their respective fields. This dream became a reality when I attended the Fletcher School.

Bill was a lively and enthusiastic lecturer. He possessed a wealth of knowledge and loved geography. He often brought to class his hand-drawn maps of the world, and would tape the maps to the classroom walls.

The most impressive things about Bill Markus were his enthusiasm and

ciple" be incorporated as part of our business plan: *"Every action we take, everything we do and say, can have an impact on the future. The actions may be small and insignificant, but they have a way of being amplified over time."* It would take me over a decade to fully comprehend and appreciate these words of wisdom. But our youth and children grantmaking focus, supported by a peace education curriculum, became two fundamental criteria for the GPBF grantmaking program.

The next critical step was for the GPBF to obtain tax-exempt status from the IRS. We intended to raise small individual donations from the general public, just like my initial $100 contribution, but without IRS approval, we would not be able to operate as a public foundation—in essence, the GPBF wouldn't be able to raise money to fulfill its mission to support organizations engaged in peace building around the world.

We submitted our application on November 20, 2010, and received the IRS approval effective January 18. It was a miraculously quick turnaround. The GPBF was now an official public foundation.

The members of our initial Board of Directors formulated the aim of the GPBF thus:

Undo the hatred, fears, and violence that

his humility. He invested his time in helping me find my way as a young college student, and did it with genuine enthusiasm that was contagious. He never talked down to me; I never felt inadequate. I strove to replicate his demeanor when I hired college interns in my CPA practice and the GPBF to work with me and offered them the opportunity to grow and learn.

have been passed down from one generation to the next, an evident root cause of violent conflict; and by breaking this cycle, contribute to the building of sustainable peace all children deserve.

And our mission statement ran as follows:

Contribute to the building of global peace by supporting organizations and projects that restore, rebuild, and transform relationships that have been broken due to prejudices, stereotyping, hatreds, and fears that may have accumulated over generations.

———

During this initial period of my new foundation, friends of mine served as role models for me on how to respond to human violence in an altruistic manner. They formed two organizations, Martha's Run and the Ken Waldie Memorial Fund, to honor and memorialize their loved ones—two individuals who had spent a significant portion of their lives serving others—and to overcome adversity, loss, pain, and suffering and turn their grief into energies to benefit the greater good. I was determined to follow their example, and their long-term efforts inspired me to do the same with the GPBF.

These organizations have been anything but a flash in the pan. Both receive steadfast community support, and at the time of this writing, Martha's Run is approaching three decades in operation, and the Waldie Fund has been going for over twenty years.

Martha's Run
Martha Dixon Martinez was an FBI agent who was killed in the line of duty on November 22, 1994.

My friends since grade school—Martha's sister Jan Dixon, her husband Terry Smith, and the rest of the Dixon family—honored Martha by establishing the Martha Fund, a charitable organization dedicated to building children's playgrounds. The primary means of raising money is Martha's Run, a challenging 10K run and 2K run-and-walk through the rolling hills of Mt. Lebanon. Martha's Run began in 1997 to honor her.

Growing up, Martha Dixon would often be found playing in the backyard with a bunch of neighborhood kids. The television show *The F.B.I.* was popular at the time, and they would play cops and robbers out there for hours. On one such occasion, someone tagged Martha, saying, "FBI, you're under arrest!"

Martha whipped around and responded, "No—FBI, *you're* under arrest!"

Kevin Dixon, Martha's older brother, says this favorite anecdote exemplified Martha's independent spirit very well. "As the sixth out of eight children, she had to fight for her place," he recalls. "She would be sticking up for herself at all times … We'd say teasingly, 'You're just a little kid, what do you know?' Martha would bristle, stand up for herself, and never back down at that kind of treatment. She demanded equality."

Martha was loyal even as a child. When she was halfway through the third grade, her school wanted to promote her to the advanced class, but she didn't want to leave her friends. When she was informed they were taking her to another class, she picked up her books and followed the nun out of the classroom. As the nun turned to open the door of her new class, Martha marched right past her to the principal's office, where she dumped her books on the desk and said, "I quit!" Martha won that day, and wasn't promoted to the advanced class until the start of the following year.

Martha joined the FBI in 1987 after working as a forensic chemist with the Arkansas State Crime Lab. An avid runner and athlete, she went on to become a technically trained agent and the first-ever female SWAT team member for the Knoxville, Tennessee, field office.

"Our family was really shocked, at first, about the turn to a law enforcement career for Martha; she was, after all, the only one to join law enforcement," says Kevin. But Martha's personality fit the FBI lifestyle, and her family came around to the idea.

In 1992, she moved to the Washington D.C. office to cover drug cases, crime, and cold cases. On November 22, 1994, a homicide suspect entered the cold case squad room of the Metropolitan Police Department headquarters where Martha was stationed and opened fire on the office.

"There's a diagram of how it happened," says Kevin. "Martha was sitting at a desk, right next to the door. The person who shot her entered, walked past her to a corner office, and started shooting. Martha got up and went to the scene instead of taking the opportunity to run. We knew Martha well enough to know that there was never a question in her mind to run. She was going to help her colleagues in the other room."

The Dixon family struggled through a mix of pride and anger about Martha's decision to stay and fight. "There's the pain of knowing she could've escaped, but chose not to. But we're proud of her for being true to who she was," says Kevin.

Through their grief, the family decided to honor Martha's life instead of focusing on her death.

"We've built joy upon the grief," says Kevin. "With the run and building playgrounds, we've really grown closer as a family. It's been a labor of love."

Today, because of Martha, more children have the opportunity to play outside and experience the outdoors. Martha's Fund has built or contributed to over twenty-five playgrounds as a testament to her love of children, which she showed to her nieces and nephews. As one of eight siblings, Martha never saw a shortage of children around at family gatherings, and she was devoted to them, taking every holiday opportunity with the FBI to go home and spend time with her many nephews and nieces.

And Martha's legacy lives on beyond the playgrounds she's helped inspire. She was awarded the FBI's Memorial Star of Valor posthumously, and Pittsburgh's South Side FBI Building is named after her. Martha has also inspired others to follow in her shoes: her niece, Kevin's daughter, decided to become a state trooper, bringing the total of Dixon family members in law enforcement to two.

The Ken Waldie Memorial Fund

This fund was established in 2002 to honor my friend and high-school classmate, Ken Waldie. Ken had also lost his life on 9/11, when American Airlines Flight 11 flew into my niece Katie's office in the World Trade Center's North Tower.

While Ken Waldie was well known for being a Naval Academy star, exceptional swimmer in high school, and fierce competitor in all things, what comes up most often with people is how valued he was as a friend.

"Kenny was everybody's best friend," says Ken's best friend Steve McGinnis, known to his friends as Mac. Mac met eleven-year-old Kenny in Little League, where he stood out not only for his baseball skills but because of how encouraging he was to all the players around him. Ken went on to become the best man at Mac's wedding.

As a senior quality control engineer at Raytheon, Ken was often referred to by colleagues as "9-1-1," because he was the engineer they called when something went wrong. He was answering one of these calls when he boarded American Airlines Flight 11 at the last minute from Boston to California on September 11, 2001.

Grieving deeply and still somewhat in shock, Mac drove up to the memorial service with five other hometown friends. At the service, Ken's family, friends, Naval Academy classmates, and Raytheon colleagues packed the house. The family had expected a large turnout, as Ken's class had been the biggest in the Naval Academy and he had been elected class president for all four years. But more came, and some people had to attend the service from the basement via remote cameras.

On the way home from the memorial, as they reminisced over childhood memories of Kenny, an idea was born to create a memorial fund for college scholarships centered around his personality traits.

The Ken Waldie Memorial Fund was established in 2002 to award scholarships to graduating high-school seniors of Bethel Park High School, Ken's alma mater, based on their demonstration of living by Ken's key traits—friendship, character, and honor.

"Initially, we went into it just trying to remember and honor Ken every day," says Mac. "We started out by sending out letters to friends and auctioning off sports tickets."

Over the years, the fund evolved to raise over $242,000 as the "Friends of Waldie," as labeled by a local journalist, were able to bring many of our Bethel Park High School community together to reconnect and to support the cause. In true Kenny fashion, the fund continuously awards the largest individual scholarships to Bethel Park High School students. The Waldie Fund has accomplished a great deal—a good example of how sustained efforts with small dollar contributions will produce lasting results.

A granite bench honoring Ken Waldie, donated by the Bethel Park High School class of 1973, now sits in the lobby of the high school's athletic building.

Mac and friends plan to dissolve the fund on the twenty-fifth anniversary of Ken's death. As it is one of the longest-standing scholarship funds at Bethel Park High School, they're proud of what Ken's memory has accomplished.

"When I think about Ken now, I have a smile on my face and peace in my heart," says Mac.

———

The members of our initial Board of Directors were an inspiration to me as well. They were extraordinarily generous with both their time and their financial donations at this startup phase of the GPBF. We were starting from scratch and operating on a shoestring budget; all our startup funding came from the board. The foundation would never have gotten off the ground without them.

But with their help, by the end of 2011—its first full year of operations—the GPBF had adopted a logo, launched a website, held its first fundraiser, and ended the year with no outstanding bills—and with money in the bank and a balance sheet that showed a positive fund balance. We got through our first year intact, and laid a rock-solid foundation for years to come. It was a magnificent start.

———

Initially, Phyllis expressed her skepticism of the likelihood of any successful outcome from peace building. "We will never have peace in this world," she said. Nonetheless, she supported me. After the launch of the GPBF, she wrote this lovely note on the inside cover of a journal she gave me on my birthday on September 30, 2010:

I hope all your dreams come true with your new foundation efforts! You are the greatest for many, many reasons—remember to laugh a lot and know that God goes with you in your journey!

So what happened? Simply put, Phyllis became a believer as the GPBF transformed from a dream to an actual entity, tangible and concrete. She'd struggled with everything while it was intangible, vague, and hard to grasp, just as many of us do. Had I not gone to the Fletcher School and studied under the tutelage of Professor Chigas, I would have been in the same boat.

But after I persevered in my goal, she grew to admire me for my vision. Around the ten-year anniversary of the founding of the GPBF, she bought me this framed quote by Albert Camus, telling me it reminded her of me:

He said, "In the midst of hate, I found there was, within me, an invincible love. In the midst of tears, I found there was, within me, an invincible smile. In the midst of chaos, I found there was, within me, an invincible calm. I realized, through it all, that in the midst of winter, I found there was, within me, an invincible summer. And that makes me happy. For it says that no matter how hard the world pushes against me, within me, there's something stronger—something better, pushing right back."

In the formative stages of my organization, Phyllis was concerned about my time commitment to the GPBF and how that would take time away from her, our family, and my moneymaking opportunities in my CPA practice. This, too, was understandable. My time away from Phyllis and our family had always been an issue in our marriage after our children were born. It stemmed from an unwritten pact: she'd become a stay-at-home mom to focus on raising our children while I'd become the sole breadwinner for our family. I'd always supplemented my income with moonlighting work for other CPA firms and my own clients, and this work had kept me away from home many evenings and weekends.

But that hard work had paid off. We were able to save enough money for a down payment on our home in Mt. Lebanon, which was a dream come true. Phyllis and I wanted to raise our family in an excellent school district, from kindergarten through high school, without having to move. Stability was a top priority for us for our children; I particularly didn't want them to live in four different houses in five years, like I had experienced growing up. We vowed to be the very best parents in the world—to provide our children with comfort, stability, and security, and most of all, with an excellent education.

The time issue had again become exacerbated after I started my own CPA practice from scratch. We went from a six-figure income to zero, practically overnight. (In the beginning I had just one client, paying me four hundred dollars per month.) For many years I worked all the time just to keep our heads above water, and Phyllis felt that she was raising our children all by herself. She resented me for not being there to help her; I resented her for not appreciating my contribution to our family and her not having to work outside of our home. And it was these resentments that would build into a new tense situation when I decided to attend the Fletcher School and found the GPBF.

Our marriage survived—partly because

Father John Rebel

Father John Rebel's last name fit him; he was a rebel. I really liked that about him. He and I liked to sit around, sip on a glass of wine, and solve all the problems of the world.

Father Rebel was a friend of the McCloskey family going back to the early 1960s. He was there when Phyllis's mother died. He married us. He baptized our three children. Instead of making us take a series of marriage classes that the Catholic church required, Father Rebel took us out to dinner, a week or so before our wedding date. Time was short—we'd planned our whole wedding in six weeks—and that dinner was our marriage class, where Phyllis and I learned about Father Rebel's secret ingredient for a long-lasting marriage.

"As time goes on," he advised us, "your life will become more complicated. You'll have work demands, stresses associated with raising your children, etc., that will make your time together scarce. You must carve out time for yourselves, to be alone together, on a regular schedule, every week. That way you will have a better chance of staying connected, of not drifting apart. You must make this the priority in your marriage life."

Father Rebel gave us the poem *DESIDERATA* for our wedding gift. We framed it, and it has followed us as we moved from Pittsburgh to Denver, from Denver to Pittsburgh, from Pittsburgh to New Orleans, and then back to Pittsburgh. Its words of wisdom have guided our life.

At a celebration event for the ten-year anniversary of my CPA practice on May 23, 2004, Father Rebel wrote we were blessed with good role models. My mother had hung in there with my dad as he suffered through bouts of depression and financial devastation; Phyllis's father had stuck by her mother as she suffered and died from alcoholism. And we also had a good spiritual advisor, a Catholic priest named Father John Rebel, who guided us through the rough patches. He taught Phyllis and me the importance of carving out time for each other throughout our life together.

But ultimately, it was our strong love and commitment to each other that kept us together.

I have never met a human being who loves as deeply as Phyllis does. She falls hard as she mourns the loss of a loved one, even her dogs—she has a hard time letting go and moving on. Never impressed with the nouveau riche, or people who flaunt their material possessions, she forever reminds me that "all that glitters is not gold," and helps me to stay grounded. She lifted me up when we first met on October 21, 1972, and has continued to lift me up over the next fifty years whenever I've been down, and as I've dealt with loss, disappointments, hurt, and sorrow. She has been my angel time and time again. I would have never made it this far in life without her.

these kind and insightful words in our autographs book:

Tommy, Tommy, Tommy—I am so glad you are so successful and thankful but how could you not succeed with the support group that you have (witnessed today) and the lively faith. Could we expect less—no!

The last time Phyllis and I saw Father Rebel was at a funeral home in December 2012. Kathleen's sister Rita had passed away, and we talked about having dinner together after the holidays. But we waited too long, and never had that dinner together. Father Rebel passed away, unexpectedly, on March 17, 2013. We really miss him—but his memory lives on.

The Reverend Pat Albright described our life together with the acronym **ABC**:

Adventure—We were bold, daring, not afraid to take on risks

Burden—We took on others' burdens by helping those in need

Covenant—We lived by an unwritten pact to always support each other

Pat was spot-on with this summary. My Fletcher School adventure was *ABC* on a grand scale—and that approach carried us through one of the most significant challenges in our marriage.

CHAPTER TWENTY
Joining a Community

n January 1994, St. Anne Church hosted a celebration event in their school gymnasium (my old sanctuary) to celebrate the one-hundred-year anniversary of the school's founding. When I attended this event, it was the first time I had set foot in the gym since the early 1970s, and I was pleased to reconnect with a friend and former classmate, Jan Dixon (now married to Terry Smith, another friend, classmate, and teammate).

As I stood there in the gym (it smelled the same) and talked to Jan, my mind took me back to when I was a fourteen-year-old eighth-grader and how safe and secure I'd felt in that place. Back then, it was a tumultuous time in my home life. Now, as a thirty-nine-year-old adult, I felt warm and fuzzy nostalgic feelings erupting inside me. In that moment, and ever since, I recognized the significance of the St. Anne School community (coaches, teachers, friends, teammates, and classmates) at that pivotal time in my life.

The community there gave me an incredible sense of belonging. I felt accepted and admired by my teammates, teachers, and coaches. Three of my eighth-grade teachers, Tom Herward, Sister Collette, and Sister Mary James, individually and privately approached me at the end of the school year and congratulated me on having a great year, and they each told me that I was a real gentleman. I ended my eighth-grade school year with many accomplishments: I was selected to play in the Catholic league basketball all-star game; my basketball teammates selected me as their captain and most valuable player; and my classmates chose me to receive the American Legion Award, a medal awarded to those who exemplify six character-defining qualities: courage, honor, leadership, patriotism, scholarship, and service.

My classmates had published the following in the St. Anne School newsletter at the end of the school year:

OUTSTANDING PERSON

Tom Etzel is one of the nicest boys in our school. Tom is friendly, courteous, considerate of others and respectful. He has been playing football since sixth grade. He is captain of the basketball team and captain of the intramural team.

He was voted most outstanding boy in the eighth grade because of his unique personality. Because of his ease in making friends, he is very popular. Tom has all the qualities of a leader and that is why we voted him the most outstanding boy in the eighth grade.

These kind words forever helped me feel good about myself and keep my head up whenever I faced harsh and mean-spirited people in the world.

And I had great mentors there too. At the core of the St. Anne School community stood a Catholic nun, Sister John Ann, who became my first angel. She was one in a million. I was blessed to have her in my life, and her steadfast love and support guided me

Sister John Ann

Drawn to her classroom after school hours, I sat across from Sister John Ann at her desk on many afternoons and talked to her about my worries.

Sister John Ann took on many additional roles beyond being a teacher: She was a confidant, a counselor, and a source of security and stability for me during a time when my home life was in upheaval. She became my rock. Most importantly, she listened as I confided in her about what was going on at home. She didn't offer me any clear-cut solutions. Instead, she sent me a steady stream of notes, full of support and encouragement.

April 13, 1968 (towards the end of seventh grade)

There has been a big improvement since the first day of school, Tom. But this improvement can't stop, it has to grow, Tommy, or else we become like "dead wood"—just existing—not living. A "real boy" doesn't just exist! He lives an active life—full of energy directed to doing what he knows is the right thing, at all times. Sometimes this is a big price for him to pay—he feels unwanted, his friends laugh at him, he feels alone— he gets mad—his temper flies—until... he realizes that it takes a guy with a lot of "guts," determination, courage to do what is right, good, Christian. Tom, that's going to be asked of you all your life. It's not going to be easy—I know— but—a real boy is NEVER A QUITTER! Stick with it, Tom—no matter how much it hurts, costs, or how hard it is!

It helps to keep "close contact" with God—talk things over with him—just tell it all to him—even when you're mad. But never, never give up, Tom. Life is too short to stop trying.

to stay on the right path. And the counseling I got from her would foreshadow my seeking help and advice from people I trusted and respected for the rest of my life. She provided a safe place for me to open up, express my inner fears, and have a voice.

Because of people like Sister John Ann, and the everlasting positive effect of experiences like my time as an eighth grader at the St. Anne School Community, community is a core value in my life. Community produces a sense of belonging; it's a place to grow, to be nourished; a place where you don't feel so alone in the world. Whoever we are, we can find places and people in this world that will do this for us.

And from the outset, I yearned for the GPBF to find a community to replicate that experience on a global scale.

———

It was essential at the beginning for the GPBF to reach out and become part of a global peace building community. We would be ineffective if we worked in a vacuum. So I recommended to the GPBF board that we consult with Professor Chigas on how best to do this, and they agreed and supported me.

On November 17, 2010, I flew to Boston and met with Professor Chigas at her office at

April 25, 1969 (towards the end of eighth grade)
...You're one guy that's really and truly GREAT. Great in the growth of character, great in the sincerity and respect you show, great in the example and influence you have shown to your classmates, and great in your simplicity. Not being a goody-good; you have developed into a boy that anyone can be proud of and proud to know. I can't help but be deeply impressed with you and your attitude. Keep them developing, Tommy.

———

the Fletcher School. She greeted me warmly with a big hug and kiss. Ever so humble, she joked apologetically about her cramped office space. Before we began our meeting, she took a phone call from her daughter, who was in her first semester at Tufts University, and they impressed me by speaking with each other in Greek.

We then got down to business. Professor Chigas shared with me some current trends in the global peace building field, including an emerging focus on peace building for women and efforts to find ways to measure program outcomes.

Our discussion then turned to the GPBF specifically: our intent to focus on youth and children's programs (similar to my thesis) and the GPBF's need to join a peace building community. She urged me to seek membership in the Alliance for Peacebuilding (AfP), based in Washington, D.C. (I learned later that AfP was a nonpartisan network of over a hundred organizations working to end violent conflict and build peace.) Professor Chigas told me that the AfP membership would be beneficial in many ways. It would provide access to others in the field; help us to determine where we fit in; show us who was doing what; and provide insight as to how we could add value. It was great advice—up to that point, I hadn't even known that AfP existed. I realized how very little I knew about the global peace building field.

AfP, incorporated in 2005, was a relatively new organization. It was apparent to me, though, that with its mission "to build sustainable peace and security worldwide," it offered the GPBF a great deal. I felt that it would be a good fit for us, so after I returned to Pittsburgh and consulted with the GPBF board, I proceeded and submitted our application for the GPBF to join AfP. The application for membership required a recommendation from two AfP members, and I was able to secure recommendations from Saji Prelis, the Director of Children and Youth Programmes for Search for Common Ground—one of my thesis case-study subjects—and Professor Chigas.

Saji wrote the following in his recommendation:

I am writing to confirm that I have become very aware of Tom Etzel and his leadership in setting up the Global Peace Building Foundation (GPBF). Its focus on investing in grassroots peace building is a key strategic entry point to strengthen local capacities for peace. I really would love to see the GPBF enable children and youth to become the positive change makers in their own communities.

Professor Chigas wrote this:

I too am writing to support the application of the Global Peace Building Foundation for membership in AfP. Tom was my student at the Fletcher School, where he became interested in peace building and has since taken extraordinary initiative to establish the Foundation and forge connections and partnerships with organizations in the field. As Saji mentioned, the focus in supporting grassroots peace building and inter-group interaction as an entry point in peace building – all in partnership with local and international peace building organizations. I think GPBF will be a good member; GPBF is anxious to forge connections with members both to help strengthen practitioners' work (both international and local partners) and to learn from them.

Our membership application was approved by the AfP Board of Directors shortly thereafter, and the GPBF entered a whole new world I'd had no idea existed—a world abundant with Fletcher School alumni.

———

I attended my first AfP conference—"Peace building 2.0: Managing Complexity and Working Across Silos"—in May of 2012. My first impression was that this peace building field was sort of a cottage industry, a loosely organized field. This was not a negative for me. In fact it was quite the opposite—I saw this as a land of opportunity.

The conference title was most fitting. This first conference served as an introduction for me into the global peace building world, where there were hundreds of attendees representing diverse backgrounds: academics, government policymakers, peace building practitioners, diplomats, and NGOs.

At the center of it all was Melanie Greenberg, the president and CEO of AfP. I wanted to greet Melanie and introduce myself, but she was surrounded by so many people, she was too busy for even a brief introduction. But I observed that she brought a remarkable positive energy to the conference.

When I departed D.C. after attending the conference, I felt like I was on the outside looking in. I didn't feel a sense of belonging to that AfP community, which seemed very big to me. I needed to find a connection. Little did I know that Melanie would become my next angel on the journey.

I first met Melanie in 2012. My son Mark, still an undergraduate at Duquesne University, accompanied me on the four-hour drive from Pittsburgh to Washington, D.C. It would be the first of several trips to D.C. that Mark and I took together. This was when I began to refer to Mark as the GPBF's Ambassador.

Mark and I met with Melanie in her

Melanie Greenberg

Melanie Greenberg has worked in peace building for almost three decades, helping shape the field from silos of conflict studies, mediation, and other areas into one unified sector. She has helped develop peace processes in the Middle East, Northern Ireland, and the Caucasus, paving the way alongside other experts for generations of peace builders.

Melanie graduated from Stanford Law School in 1990, as the Berlin Wall came down. It was a formative phase for global geopolitics, and a time of reckoning for the new field of peace building. "When I was coming up through college, there was no field of peace building," she says. Asked how she decided on peace building as a career, she shares, "I didn't start in any one place. I think peace building is a calling."

Melanie traces that calling back to her early days in law school. "One summer in law school, I worked on prisoner death row cases in Georgia," she recalls. "Seeing the defendants—how they lived, what brought them to their crimes—and hearing their families' stories got me thinking, *There's more to this than we know.* I don't know if the Georgia trials influenced what I did in law school, but they did open me up to this interdisciplinary focus on conflict."

Upon graduating, she worked at Stanford's Center for International Security and Cooperation for two years before joining the William and Flora Hewlett Foundation, where she managed peace building grants.

Soon after, Melanie transitioned to focus on researching issues of justice in post-conflict peace building at John Hopkins School for Advanced International Studies as a Visiting Scholar.

office on the morning of November 19. She gave us a warm and friendly welcome. After brief introductions, Melanie began the meeting with a question: "So what brought you into the peace building field?"

I started to respond but hesitated, and decided to let Mark answer the question.

"My cousin, Katie McCloskey, was killed on 9/11," Mark told her. "She was on the ninety-seventh floor of the North Tower when the first hijacked plane flew into the building."

Melanie responded with a deep sigh, visibly shaken. Mark and I remarked to each other after the meeting how we could feel her compassion and empathy at that moment; we could tell she shared in our sorrow and grief.

This was the first of many meetings and discussions I had with Melanie. I recall telling her that we felt isolated in Pittsburgh; I even brought up the idea of exploring the prospect of subleasing office space in Washington, D.C. as an "in-kind" contribution to help us find our way in the global peace building community. Melanie opened the door and welcomed me into her home—and, in a sense, into the AfP community. She was accessible; she was generous with her time; she willingly shared her knowledge and expertise with me. She held my hand and guided me as I

Later, she took a position as the President for Alliance for Peacebuilding (AfP), an organization that was initially a grantee during her time at the Hewlett Foundation. Alliance for Peacebuilding allowed her to develop an international community of organizations.

"Growing the membership took a lot of time in those early years, but finally AfP developed a policy voice that brought a peace building perspective to policy," she says.

Under her leadership, AfP grew from thirty member organizations to one hundred, developed an internationally renowned annual peace conference, and shepherded in a culture of locally led peace building efforts.

After seven years, she migrated to Humanity United as its Managing Director of Peacebuilding and Conflict Transformation, where she works today to infuse a local approach to the organization's efforts.

Despite being a leading force developing the field, Melanie remains humbly convinced she has more to learn. "I think this has to be a field where you're incredibly humble," she says. "You're dealing with people at the worst point in their entire lives, at the issue that is central to them. You're going to say the wrong thing from time to time, and people will correct you. You have to be comfortable with that."

She continues to contribute her own wisdom about peace building as a writer, lecturer, teacher, and trainer for numerous entities like congressional staffers, scientists at the National Institutes of Health, international lawyers, business executives, and graduate students.

"I've gotten so much from my peers," she says. "I am so inspired by the searched. How to expand our following, how to bring others into the fold, how to increase our funding—we needed help navigating these murky waters. But Melanie and I shared that common thread: we were people who cared about this world and wanted to make it a better place. She became a good friend and mentor for me.

At our November 19 meeting, Melanie first mentioned that the GPBF should look into the Peace and Security Funders Group (PSFG). She told me that PSFG would provide good networking opportunities with the global peace and security philanthropic community. She and I then had follow-up meetings throughout 2013, when I purposely arranged my trips to Washington, D.C. around her schedule so that we could continue our dialogue, and I could keep her abreast of the GPBF's progress.

On Sunday, January 26, 2014, I drove to Washington, D.C., in a snowstorm to meet with Melanie the following morning. I wanted to talk to her more about the PSFG, and it was a worthwhile trip. She recommended that the GPBF join the PSFG, and said she would submit an introductory letter on our behalf to Alexandra Toma, the organization's new executive director.

Melanie followed up on her commit-

optimism and intense creativity and generosity you need to do this work...I hope I've helped to build the field, and I root for everyone I've ever worked with."

ment. This introduction was instrumental, as PSFG accepted the GPBF as a member on April 18, 2014—and Alex Toma was a gem in the application process. She warmly welcomed us, even though we were such a small foundation. We were by far the smallest foundation ever to join PSFG—but that didn't matter to Alex. It was the GPBF's grantmaking that mattered. And this, in turn, would affect how the GPBF gave consideration to grant requests from small startup peace building projects all over the world.

We were so excited! This was a milestone for the GPBF. We issued a press release informing the public about the PSFG network of public, private, and family foundations and individual philanthropists, and how our membership in the PSFG would help the GPBF become more effective in its peace building efforts.

———

I attended the PSFG Annual Conference, held in Chicago, a week after the GPBF became a member. My major takeaway from the conference was the realization that this friendly and warm community of philanthropists really believes that the work they're doing is important and that they are making a difference to make the world a better place.

Alexandra Toma

Alexandra Toma and the GPBF first crossed paths in 2014. Alex was starting out as the new executive director for the Peace and Security Funders Group (PSFG), and the GPBF had just applied to become the group's newest member. In reviewing the GPBF's application, Alex asked me if our $500 average grant size was a typo. She'd thought it was intended to be $50,000. When I assured her it was accurate, she didn't skip a beat before accepting the GPBF as a member.

"I don't treat any of the members differently—whether they're massive or giving out micro-grants," says Alex emphatically. "We lived above a garage when I came to America. There were actual cars underneath. And when I went to the grocery store with my mom, who has a thick Romanian accent, people would always ask, 'Where are you from? No, where are you *really* from?' I prefer to treat everyone equally."

Born in the communist dictatorship of Romania and raised on Long Island, in New York, Alex had a childhood that revolved around the desire for peace and security. Her mother Rina fled Romania in 1982, after getting a tourist visa to visit her brother in Germany; in Germany, she petitioned for political asylum at every embassy she could find and was eventually granted a visa to the United States. It was a year before she could send for her two daughters—who were only three and one years old when she left—through the U.S. family reunification program.

"Justice is a part of my DNA," says Alex, recalling family dinner-table conversations that ranged from which family member had disappeared to who had

The positivity and confidence—and non-arrogance—displayed at that first PSFG conference reminded me of our first two years at the GPBF, when many on our board embraced Margaret Mead's famous quote: *"Never doubt that a small group of thoughtful, committed citizens can change the world; indeed, it's the only thing that ever has."*

As I gazed around the conference room at all those big players in philanthropy, it took me back to the Western Pennsylvania Summer Basketball Camp, a high-school basketball camp I attended in June 1970 and again the following June at Gannon College in Erie, Pennsylvania. The Camp was directed by the legendary high-school basketball coach Edward McCluskey. When I'd walked into the gymnasium for the first time, I was awestruck—the gym was much bigger than any I'd ever played in up to that point in my life. And the Camp was loaded with talented players who came from all over the region: Ohio, Washington, D.C., Pennsylvania, and New York. At five feet, four inches, I was the shortest player on the court—all the other players towered over me. But I found my place on that court, as I was quick and nimble, and the coaches voted me as the runner-up for the Most Improved Player award.

had their home demolished. "It was never a choice to *not* be involved in peace and security."

It seemed natural that when Alex grew up, she would set out to build a career in foreign policy. She started out as a foreign policy and defense advisor in the U.S. Congress, but soon grew frustrated with politics getting in the way of good policy.

"Then I found philanthropy, and it was like, 'I get to do the peace and security piece while mobilizing resources to help people?'" she recalls.

Under Alex's leadership, the PSFG tripled their membership and their programs expanded significantly. Today, part of her job is to entice funders to invest in peace and security issues—only one percent of all grantmaking goes towards this sector, according to a study by Candid, an information service specializing in reporting on U.S. nonprofits. She points out that these are front-page issues in newspapers globally—from war in the Middle East to atrocities in Southeast Asia to domestic unrest here in America.

"It's hard to prove that you're making an impact when what you're doing is stopping something really horrible from happening," she says.

Despite these challenges, Alex and PSFG are making a demonstrable difference and have earned a reputation as trusted partners and thought-leaders. In 2021, Alex was asked to advise the Biden-Harris presidential transition team on increasing diversity, equity, and inclusion efforts within U.S. government agencies working on peace and security.

When crisis struck in Afghanistan after the government's fall and the Taliban takeover in August 2021, PSFG

Similarly, PSFG opened a whole new world for me—a world of philanthropy dedicated to peace and security. We now belonged to a small, close-knit community. And as I had done when I was the shortest player on my basketball team, I dedicated myself to improving as much I could. I immersed myself in everything PSFG offered: education, collaboration, best practices.

The PSFG team, led by Alex, instituted many small group meetings, both in person and virtually, that helped me get to know most of the community members. I was able to build personal relationships with many of them based on trust, respect, and confidentiality. And I have attended every PSFG Annual Conference since that first one in 2014. The 2016 conference in Portland, Oregon, was especially noteworthy, as the GPBF was spotlighted in the very first edition of the PSFG's Peace and Security Funding Index Report.

Alex was instrumental in giving the GPBF this special recognition, and she has been a mentor and genuine friend to me ever since we first met in April 2014. She has been a blessing to me—another angel in my midst, accompanying me on my journey.

was able to coordinate a call for over eighty-five funders and the White House. After the January 6 insurrection at Capitol Hill in Washington D.C., PSFG convened members for a discussion centered on how to preserve democracy in the U.S. Whatever situation arises, PSFG makes an effort to bring philanthropies to the table to build a rapid, cohesive response.

"With PSFG, I get to shape the way all of these people think about their role in altruism and philanthropy," she says. That ability to pave the path that foundations, institutes, and philanthropists follow in peace and security funding is what keeps Alex in the field.

CHAPTER TWENTY-ONE

You Believe It When You See It

Phyllis accompanied me on two due-diligence visits to GPBF grantees PeacePlayers International (PPI-NI) in Belfast, Northern Ireland, and Seeds of Peace (SOP) in Otisfield, Maine. Both PPI-NI and SOP were the subjects of case studies in my Fletcher School thesis, and they later became the GPBF's first two grantees.

These visits provided us with an insight into the lived experiences of youth and children in their respective communities. My belief, attained during my thesis interviews, that sustainable peace is built on personal relationships and that person-to-person activities and outreach done at the local level can succeed in transforming lives broken by prejudice, stereotyping, hatred, and fear, was further solidified during these visits.

These visits were also Phyllis's first exposure to grassroots peace building, and with them she shed her skepticism and became open to the possibility that this work, done by ordinary citizens, could be the springboard steps to building sustainable peace in the world.

BELFAST, NORTHERN IRELAND

Phyllis and I spent a week with PPI-NI in Belfast in May 2013 to get an up-front-and-close sense of the area's culture and the history of the conflict there. She and I were aware that a fragile peace had existed since the Good Friday Agreement was signed on April 10, 1998.

The Good Friday Agreement had put an end to the most recent violent period known as "The Troubles," a thirty-year period characterized by bombings, police clashes with protestors, and guerilla warfare.

As Phyllis and I walked the streets with tour guides and drove throughout the city with talkative taxi drivers, the tensions that remain under the surface were brought to light. Signs of the three-hundred-year conflict between Catholic nationalists and Protestant loyalists are ever-present. Neighborhoods distinguished by flags and murals are physically separated by "peace walls"—thirty-foot-high walls of concrete and steel chain-link fence. The newest peace wall went up as recently as 2002. The walls have been turned into artworks of commemoration, nationalist and loyalist pride, and dark warnings. Our taxi driver pointed out all the Ulster Union and British flags marking the territory as we drove through the Shankill neighborhood.

As we met and talked with the PPI-NI staff, we learned that ninety-four percent of schools in Northern Ireland are still segregated. PPI-NI works with twenty different schools to bring students from different sides onto the same basketball courts.

Phyllis and I visited a couple of gymnasiums that integrated Catholic and Protestant students by teaching them basic basketball skills such as dribbling and shooting. The basketball programs were supplemented with experiential learning sessions about prejudice, sectarianism, and peer pressure. In these programs, young people learn how it feels to be discriminated against. (One of our most significant observations was how a couple of the Catholic boys answered "No" to the question, "Is the act of Catholic boys throwing rocks at a Protestant boy's bus sectarianism?" The rationale of their answer was based on their experience that Protestant boys threw rocks at *their* bus.)

Megan Lynch, an American Fellow working on PPI-NI's staff for one year, explained to us how PPI's peace education curriculum is woven into each school's personal development and mutual-under-standing curriculum. The teachers rely on PPI to answer the young students' questions about sectarianism, thinking that PPI is better prepared to address the topic.

We also had the opportunity to meet with Trevor Ringland (who assisted me in my thesis) during the organization's "Spring Jam" basketball tournament. He commented, "We work on peace every day."

Trevor shared his story with me. He's a partner at Macaulay and Ritchie Solicitors, one of Northern Ireland's leading law firms, and the Chairman of the Board of Directors for PeacePlayers Northern Ireland. But he's also the son of a Northern Ireland policeman, and one of Ireland's most famous former rugby players—two backgrounds that have spurred him on to become a voluntary peace builder.

When Trevor was twelve, he was searching for a pencil when he found photos of maimed men and women, burned in a bomb attack. He never forgot what he'd seen, and even though his parents worked hard to give him a normal childhood, the conflict kept rearing its head.

"We lived a normal life growing up, it was just in abnormal circumstances," he says, launching into stories about the times he and his family lived out of the police station in Larne. "We came out of the police station one night, and the IRA appeared and started shooting. My father dived under a car, and a gunfight went on for two hours. Meanwhile, my mother got a call saying that homes of police families were being attacked. This happened the same night."

Trevor's father, Adrian, would go on to check his police car for bombs each morning, and his mother would check to see if anyone was at the door before leaving home each day. As a police family, they didn't just receive threats from the IRA, but also from Protestants who considered them too protective of Catholics.

This made it impossible for Adrian to watch his son's rugby games from the family section in the stands. Instead, he'd watch from a distant corner—in disguise. This didn't stop him from cheering on the team, though. Nor did it stop him from calling out referees when they made a poor call.

"My father took out the stress on rugby referees," says Trevor with a half-smile. "They were a bit of a counseling service for him."

As Trevor grew up, his rugby talent earned him spots on some of Ireland's most competitive teams. On the rugby pitch, whether you were Protestant or Catholic mattered little compared with whether you were a great team player. In 1985, he led Ireland to defeat England, Wales, France, and Scotland in a Five Nations rugby championship.

Trevor took his experiences working across religious divides on the field into his professional life, working to build a campaign on creating a genuinely shared future with One Small Step, lending his now-famous name to peace building efforts, and collaborating with the American Ireland Fund to identify peace projects to fund. It was the last of these that led him to PeacePlayers International, an organization that uses sports to build a global youth movement for peace and equity.

"PeacePlayers is such a simple example of how things can be different in Northern Ireland, Cyprus, the Middle East, North Africa, Rwanda, and the U.S. as well," Trevor says. "It shows that the norm can be challenged so that barriers are broken down, teachers and parents get involved, and then it has a wider impact on the local community … this is the impact."

Trevor has been the board chair of PeacePlayers Northern Ireland since 2009, and has seen the program's students grow from children to adults. One of the Belfast communities he's seen change is a neighborhood where a Protestant primary school and a Catholic primary school sat on opposing sides of the same road.

"The first time we brought [the kids] together, they had to travel in separate buses to a neutral venue," Trevor recalls. "Some parents even tried going to their lawyers to get it stopped. And then, within ten minutes, we had them running together. They were completely mixed."

Now the schools travel to practices in the same bus, the kids play on mixed teams, and their parents attend games together.

"Maybe I took too many kicks to the head, but it's the right thing to do as well," says Trevor, talking about how long it took to get Northern Ireland and PeacePlayers to where it is today.

Despite the region's history of conflict, Trevor remains a firm believer that Northern Ireland's citizens want peace. "All I have ever experienced across the island of Ireland were people who were welcoming," he says. "We got relationships so badly wrong the last hundred years, let's get them right the next hundred."

We also had the opportunity to spend time with Gareth Harper, the managing director of PPI-NI. Gareth told me that over the years, he has seen several of the organization's alumni go on to careers in human rights law, conflict transformation, and various other fields due to their involvement with PPI-NI.

"Every day, I witness the power of young people who push this place towards a better, more shared future," he said. "I have been close to tears of pride and joy on numerous occasions." One such individual is Naimh, who joined PPI-NI when it first started programming in Northern Ireland back in 2002 and worked her way through the tiers to become a current coach. Naimh's Catholic primary school existed in the middle of a Protestant neighborhood and was subject to picketing and protests.

PPI-NI worked with Naimh's school and the neighborhood's Protestant school, a mere fifty yards away, to build a primary school twinning program. Primary school twinning is the foundation of

PPI-NI's cross-community intervention. The program engages children aged nine to eleven and pairs a maintained (predominantly Catholic) primary school with a controlled (predominantly Protestant) primary school for ninety-minute sessions during the school day.

"Naimh is a real PPI-NI success story," Gareth told us. "At PPI-NI, we are working to create hundreds of Niamhs, who in turn work with thousands of Catholic and Protestant young people across Northern Ireland to bridge divides, develop leaders, and change perceptions."

As we departed to return to Pittsburgh, we were full of excitement and optimism about the future of Belfast and Northern Ireland. And we realized that it is going to take generations to transform that part of the world into a more peaceful environment. PPI-NI is one organization that is working at the grassroots level with youth and children to affect their attitudes and to shape their perceptions differently than prior generations have done.

OTISFIELD, MAINE

Phyllis and I visited the Seeds of Peace (SOP) international peace camp in the summer of 2012. Eva Gordan Armour arranged our visit, and we were greeted and escorted by Bobbi, a friendly SOP staff member.

Nestled on the shores of Pleasant Lake, the camp has the look, at first glance, of an ordinary traditional summer camp, with a beach, soccer fields, basketball courts, housing units, and a dining hall. The camp serves as the programming foundation for SOP, and is designed to be a holistic and powerful human experience. For ninety minutes of intense dialogue each day, the participants discuss and share their pain, anger, fear, hatred, and other core issues of conflict. These dialogue sessions are supervised by SOP trained facilitators. Recreational and team-building activities, like at a summer camp, balance the remainder of each day.

The young people, fourteen to fifteen years of age, are chosen by their respective governments, typically through the Ministry of Education. The governments must give consent for the young people to participate. Thousands apply, but only three hundred applicants are selected, through an extensive series of exams, essays, and interviews, to represent their countries. The young people come as mini-ambassadors from their respective countries, and there is much prestige involved.

As Phyllis and I strolled through the camp, several participants came up to us to share their transformational experiences.

Upon Rihanna's arrival from Afghanistan, she shared the apprehension of others, yet she felt open to these sharing and learning experiences. "The camp helps us to change our mind and to see other people from the other side, and to make new friends for ourselves," she told us.

Mati from India told us, "When people from home tell us that we can't get along with people from the other side, I am going to show them a picture of all of us together."

Hadi from Palestine said, "I am going to try to treat everyone how SOP treated me."

We were equally inspired by the dedicated counselors working at the camp.

Moose, from Egypt, attended the camp six years prior. Now back as a camp counselor, he reflected on what he'd learned. "As a younger man coming here, meeting the other side—a lot of Israelis, Jordanians, and Americans—it was a different experience, because you actually get a chance to be friends, and live with them for three weeks," he said. "You listen to what they have to say, they listen to what you have to say, you get to engage in dialogue and talk about it, and then run around on the same soccer team playing the same sport."

A bunk counselor shared this observation: "There's so many small moments—like brushing your teeth together that first night when campers first get there—when you see the discomfort. Then the last night, they are clinging to one another, not being able to let go."

As Phyllis and I drove back to Pittsburgh, we were mindful of the challenges these young people would face when they returned to their home countries and were again confronted with the bitterness of conflict. We were comforted to know that year-round regional programming exists in their home countries and acts as a support system. For instance, Israeli and Palestinian graduate participants, referred to as Seeds, meet throughout the year in small dialogue groups to continue to listen with respect and tolerance to the opinions of the people on the opposing side of the conflict. Other opportunities for Seeds to build on their transformational experience at the camp and further their development as leaders and advocates for peace include local workshops, community outreach efforts, community service projects, regional seminars, and global summits.

And I reflected again on Eva Gordan Armour's powerful revelation that she'd shared with me during my thesis research. Eva had been working as a counselor at the SOP international peace camp, and within a week's time, a young Israeli woman had befriended a young Palestinian man at the camp. The young Israeli woman came to Eva one evening and was sobbing, hysterical. She explained that her Palestinian friend's cousin had been shot by Israeli soldiers in the West Bank, and had died. The woman cried out, "You don't understand, this isn't just another Palestinian, this is my friend."

"It was at that moment that I realized the power of just knowing someone," Eva had told me. "And it doesn't become *them*; it becomes *my friend*, it becomes *this person*—another human being. And it is those very human experiences, those human encounters, that change us. It changed me ... it's changed you."

"The young Israeli woman was remarkable," she had continued. "She stuck through it, and she has been involved in a number of peace building efforts and is currently getting a PhD in peace building, now eleven years later. Ultimately, this is what will bring about real change in these countries."

CHAPTER TWENTY-TWO
The Critical Role of Mentors and Coaches

The "little things"—words of encouragement from a coach, a mentor's investment of time, sincere interest shown, a pat on the back, unsolicited but meaningful advice, positive feedback—can turn into big things. Many little things shaped and impacted my life, guided and lifted me up when I was down, and ultimately propelled me to establish the GPBF to help the world's youth and children.

In the formative years of the GPBF, I frequently traveled to Washington, D.C. and met with Brendan Tuohey, the co-founder of PPI. Mark accompanied me on one of my trips. Our discussions always took place at Brendan's austere PPI headquarters office.

PPI represents the ideal GPBF grantee: Contact Theory with an underlying peace education curriculum; local community–led, with low-cost fiscally responsible operations; and an emphasis on mentors and coaches.

Brendan built PPI from scratch, initially starting a basketball program in South Africa and then expanding to Cyprus, Northern Ireland, the Middle East, and the United States. Drawn to his knowledge and experience, I sought his advice, and he gave me tips on fundraising, seeking government funding, utilizing volunteers, and saving costs. He and I immediately hit it off—we shared a passion for the game of basketball, and it impressed me that he'd played at a major college level.

We both believed in combining sports with Contact Theory. He told me emphatically, "There's no better strategy than sport to reach a large number of people—reach them while they're young, and their perceptions are still changing. Our goal is to reverse these patterns of prejudice, hate, and not knowing the other that permeates the older generations in these areas of conflict. When you see someone as a human being, you are freer to act."

Brendan shared with me PPI's underlying peace education curriculum, based on the book, *The Anatomy of Peace,* written by the Arbinger Institute. He and I both understood the value of local community involvement and wholeheartedly supported such efforts. He told me, "The real key implementors of all this are people that are from these communities, that these kids know, that have had similar backgrounds, that they trust and are going to be there for the long term."

But it was Brendan's recognition of the importance of mentors— "Once you have the right people as mentors, their power and influence is incredible, the kids will look up to them"—that really hit home with me.

———

Brendan's comment reminded me of my own friend and mentor, Tim Stack, who was in a class all by himself.

Tim was always there for me. Our friendship originated at Bethany College, where Tim was in his final year when he started dating Phyllis's friend Mary Malia, who was a freshman. He left a strong impression on me the first time I met him: he was very handsome, with an air of confidence and genuineness about him. And he appeared quite a bit older, in the sense of maturity, than Phyllis, Mary, Kathleen, and me.

Tim was the big man on campus at Bethany: well known and well liked. When I learned that he had been the president of the student body at one point in his college career at Bethany, I wasn't surprised.

I could tell that he had innate leadership qualities.

Tim took me under his wing very early on. He offered advice, and I was all ears. Although we were only a few years apart in age, he was way ahead of me in the game of life, and always seemed to always be a step ahead of the crowd. He had great vision—he could see things that others would never see. He was very perceptive and could really read people. And he was without a doubt the most optimistic and positive person I ever met. His father died when he was only seven years old, which shaped his life. He had a strong sense of responsibility in his work and in his family life, and I really looked up to him.

After he graduated from Bethany College, Tim attended Virginia Commonwealth University, where he earned a master's degree in hospital administration. It didn't take him very long to get his first CEO position with a small Pittsburgh hospital, which he got when he was twenty-eight years old. I was always in awe of the fact that he interacted with physicians and board members so much older than him. He really carried himself well.

In 1987, Tim appeared as Young Administrator of the Year on the cover of *Modern Healthcare*. He later told me that this was not just a random event—that the selection was competitive, and he had worked hard at getting selected. If you really want something in life, he told me, you have to go after it—and I remembered that when I persisted in seeking admission to the Fletcher School.

Tim's appearance in *Modern Healthcare* was the launchpad for his rise in prominence in the healthcare field in the United States. He held CEO positions with big healthcare systems in Kalamazoo and Atlanta. One evening, Phyllis and I were watching PBS, and lo and behold, Tim Stack was on television in an interview with the former Surgeon General of the United States, C. Everett Koop. We weren't surprised at how confident and articulate Tim was in the interview.

Tim always told me that he didn't expect to live a long life. One of his favorite songs was "Only the Good Die Young" by Billy Joel, and one of his favorite expressions, going back to the Bethany College days, was "no game for snails." He lived his life with a sense of urgency; he didn't wait. He lived a full life in the time that he was on this earth. I remembered that, too, when I went full steam ahead after gaining admission to the Fletcher School. I felt that I had no time to waste either—and it was with Tim's example in mind that I didn't hesitate to launch the GPBF immediately after finishing my studies.

Over the years, Tim showed me the importance of words—the impact they can have. And his constant stream of positive words to me affected me in a profound way. He picked me up when I was down; he gave me encouragement when I was discouraged or disappointed. At my daughter Katie's wedding on July 31, 2010, he said to me, "You have grown so much. You are really comfortable in your own skin."

Tim died two years later, almost to the day, on July 30, 2012. He died within seven weeks of being diagnosed with cancer, at only sixty years old.

Two years after Tim's passing, I met with a psychic medium named Jennifer. I had never done this before, so I didn't have any expectations, other than I was hoping she would be able to connect me with Angel Katie. Instead, she connected me with Tim Stack.

I met Jennifer in the living room of her home. When I arrived and entered her home, she greeted me and I sat down on a couch directly across from her. She went right to work, describing names coming through to her at the beginning of the session: Robert, Tim, Mary, Margie. Tim's formal name was Robert Timothy. Mary, of course, was Tim's wife, and Margie was Tim's mother. Next, she mentioned that the loved one, Tim, had suffered intense, excruciating pain in the abdominal area before his death. Jennifer was describing his cancer.

At this moment, I realized that Jennifer had to be the real deal.

Jennifer communicated several messages from Tim to me that included love and encouragement. She told me that Tim sent his blessing to me, along with this message: "I am here to support you; you have a lot of time left, and I will greet you when you pass. You were one of the best friends I ever had ... I could always confide in you. We will have a lot of fun together when you join me ... we will be able to play golf anywhere we want to!"

I waited until I saw Mary in person to share this experience with her. She and I attended an American Ireland Fund fundraising event in Pittsburgh a few years later, and I didn't get very far into the story before I broke down and sobbed. Mary cried along with me.

I miss Tim, and Phyllis and I think of him often.

———

Brendan also spoke about the importance of coaches: "The kids will go through the leadership development programs, become assistant coaches and facilitators. They are the ones who will be your coaches long-term, and then you're expanding the number of kids and places you want to be. That is where you want to be, because these kids have lived this their whole lives."

His words elicited a memory of two coaches who came into my young life, lifted me up, and provided a springboard for my self-confidence, character growth, development, and future accomplishments for the rest of my life.

The first of these was Denny Phillips, my eight-grade football coach. He gave me a chance, and by doing so, provided me with a character-building experience that paid dividends for the rest of my life. He stressed hard work, discipline, and building what he called "intestinal fortitude." I never heard a word of profanity from him. My parents made me sit out my seventh-grade season because we didn't have health insurance, and tried to make me sit out my eighth-grade season for the same reason—but this was when I first discovered that I had a voice. Feeling suddenly empowered, I told them that I was going to play anyway. That feeling of empowerment would thrust me forward for the rest of my life; from that point forward I didn't let things get in my way. And Coach Philips was there to encourage its beginnings.

It took me half the eighth-grade season to get up to speed, but Coach Phillips didn't give up on me. He kept teaching me and encouraging me, and I got more and more playing time as the season progressed. I never left the field for the final game of the season.

Joe Quaquarucci, or "Mr. Q," my eighth-grade basketball coach, was another great influence who showered me with praise and positive feedback that helped me build my self-confidence. My heart was set on playing basketball for the St. Anne School eighth-grade team at an early age, and I started playing with the older kids in my neighborhood when I was in fourth grade. By eighth grade, I could dribble with either hand, go to the right or the left with ease, and make layup shots with both hands. Mr. Q immediately took notice, and he praised me in front of the whole team. We lost several games that season, but you would never know it from Mr. Q's behavior: he was a class act, both as a coach and as a human being.

I never had as positive a coach as Mr. Q—ever. He was a great role model, on and off the basketball court. He never talked down to us, instead remaining steadfast in his encouragement and enthusiasm. He allowed us to learn the fundamentals of the game, play hard, and have a lot of fun along the way. (We were kids, after all, and he never forgot that.) And he was in great physical condition. He scrimmaged with us without missing a beat, and could even outrun some of my teammates. He displayed good sportsmanship while being very competitive, and he showed respect. He never complained to the referees, instead focusing his time and attention during the games on coaching us. If you ever sat next to him during a game, you couldn't help but feel the boundless energy within his body. His legs and arms flailed all over the place, often knocking into you; you'd often hear him shout out, "One time, one time!" as he cheered on a teammate who'd just released a shot, trying to coax the ball into the hoop.

Mr. Q. attended almost every one of our six eighth-grade school reunions, from 1994 to our fifty-year reunion in 2019. And just as impressive, he refereed basketball and volleyball until he was ninety years old. My friend Terry Smith and I once took Mr. Q to a high-school basketball playoff game in the winter of 2019, and people there treated him liked a celebrity. So many people came up to him to say hello and give him their regards. As we watched the game, he leaned over to me and pointed out a player he considered a showboat: "Look at that player, Tommy, what a hot dog!" Mr. Q. had never gone for that showboat style of play, teaching us to be humble on and off the court.

But the term he'd used was ironic: over the final few years of his life, I and my grade-school pals Terry Smith, Michael Fahey, and George Owens occasionally met Mr. Q for lunch—at his favorite hot dog shop.

———

The quintessential mentor, Tim Stack, and my extraordinary eighth-grade coaches, Denny Phillips and Mr. Q, continue to be in the forefront of my mind as I lead the GPBF in finding and supporting grantees. We look for leaders who possess those mentors' qualities and have the capability to help transform the lives of youth and children all over the world.

As a tribute to Tim Stack, Denny Phillips, and Mr. Q, I, in turn, am now functioning in an advisory capacity as a mentor/coach to startup peace building organizations by sharing ideas and best practices from other successful grantees. It's the least I can do to honor my own mentors and return the favor they did me—by paying it forward.

———

CHAPTER TWENTY-THREE
Reach Beyond Yourself

W e must focus on the needs of others, and engage in efforts to serve others, to make the world a better place. That means getting beyond our individual ego, beyond the strong tendency to seek recognition, and beyond being self-absorbed. By doing this, we increase our awareness of the suffering in the world: in our local communities, in our country, beyond its borders, and in all the other continents. This becomes possible with an altruistic mindset.

Dr. S. Allen Foster, a Presbyterian minister, gave me a piece of advice that planted a seed that would blossom over a decade later at the outset of my peace building journey.

I first met Dr. Foster in September of 1993, when Phyllis and I decided to leave the Catholic church and join the Southminster Presbyterian Church, located in Mt. Lebanon. Dr. Foster was Senior Pastor of Southminster Church at the time, and he and I developed a close relationship over the next ten-plus years. He asked me to serve the church in various capacities, including on its Board of Trustees, Capital Campaign, Nominating Committee, and Stewardship Commission. I became an Ordained Elder of the church, and I was honored to serve. I was especially glad to help him, considering what he did for me and my family.

Dr. Foster went out of his way to serve the congregation. When I started my CPA practice in November 1993, I struggled through the time it took to build the practice. Out of the blue, in the summer of 1994, I received a call from Dr. Foster, inviting me to lunch. When we met, he asked me how things were going in my practice. I told him the truth: we were in dire financial straits. I sensed that he already knew this, as he tended to keep his ear close to the ground. He offered to help, saying the Church had a special fund to help families who were in our situation. I thanked him but declined the help, telling him that I would just stick with it. I was hopeful that in time, things would turn around. And happily, they did.

At that same lunch, Dr. Foster shared a belief with me that I will always remember. He told me, "You have to get beyond yourself." He was basically saying that I wouldn't find success in my practice until I focused on my clients' needs instead of my own. My CPA practice took on a whole new meaning when I began to view it as a ministry serving the needs of others.

Those words, *You have to get beyond yourself,* serve me today as a guidepost on my global peace building journey. Whenever I creep back into letting personal interests get in the way of my altruistic aspirations for the world at large, I remind myself that pure altruism has no strings attached.

———

On January 25, 2011, I made my very first public presentation about the GPBF. It was at my church's Tuesday-evening dinner/lecture program, *Tuesday Night Live.* My daughter Katie helped me with the technology, and we were able to include some footage of the conflict in Belfast to supplement my presentation.

It appeared that the presentation was well received, and for the most part, it was. There were many substantive questions of interest. Bill Markus and Rev. Pat Albright made brief speeches endorsing me and the GPBF, and the Reverend Ken White closed the evening with a laying of hands—a ritual in which my fellow church members gathered around me, placed their hands on my shoulder, bowed their heads, and joined Ken in prayer as he conferred a spiritual blessing on me and the GPBF: "Patient persistence in love bears fruit." I remembered those words, and they've helped me through the many obstacles I've encountered along my journey.

But not everyone was convinced. Afterwards, Pat Albright told me that one church member commented to him immediately after the laying of hands, "Where did you find this guy? He's crazy!" Another church member told me, "You should focus on peace building in this country. We really don't care about what's happening in other parts of the world." Yet another church member tried to discourage me, saying, "You're wasting your time. We only care about what's happening here in Mt. Lebanon."

These negative sentiments, expressed by a few church members, represented a microcosm of a larger community with the need to get not just beyond themselves, but beyond their local community and their own country as well. And the experience illustrated an important takeaway from my initial reading period at the Fletcher School, that is, how individualism can be a detriment to the greater good, an antithesis to altruism.

The negative feedback I received was a harbinger of dismal financial support from the congregation. On average, only one percent of the church members would ever donate money to the GPBF. This has been terribly disappointing to me, considering that they pray about breaking down the walls that separate us, tearing down the fences of hatred and indifference, overcoming our prejudices and fears, and opening ourselves to others. Yet ninety-nine percent don't convert those prayers to action, even when it is handed to them on a silver platter in the form of the GPBF mission, which aligns directly with those prayers.

———

In the spring of 2012, I participated in a two-day symposium in Chicago entitled, "Restoring Hope—Altruistic Responses to Violence." The symposium was run by Notre Dame University and funded by the Fetzer Institute, a non-profit organization based in Kalamazoo; all my travel and hotel expenses were covered by Fetzer.

A significant number of the participants, like me, had lost loved ones on 9/11, and they had responded in an altruistic manner. Many had established foundations to memorialize their loved ones. Like me, it seemed that many of them were seeking recognition or publicity for the work they were doing.

A little over four years later, I was still struggling with that goal of recognition—that is, with my ego—but I was in a better place to heed Barack Obama's advice. In a Facebook post, he had written about how he'd become frustrated as a representative in the Illinois state legislature, that he wasn't getting a lot done there, and how, when he first ran for the United States Congress in 1999, how he'd lost badly in the election. He'd wondered if maybe this was something he wasn't cut out to do. But what got him through that moment of doubt, and any other time afterward when he felt stuck, was to remind himself that it's about the work, not about himself. It wasn't about whether he was succeeding, being appreciated, feeling frustrated, or feeling stuck—because in the end, if you keep it about the work, you'll always have a path.

———

CHAPTER TWENTY-FOUR
It's Supposed to Be Hard

When I met Kathleen Rooney in 1972, her father was the president of the Pittsburgh Steelers. This was when the Steelers began their ascent to becoming the professional football dynasty they would later become, winning four Super Bowl championships in six years.

Mr. Rooney had become famous over the years for his "teaching moments." When Phyllis was in high school, he taught her how to downhill ski. Mr. Rooney was impressed by her fearlessness, and from that point forward, he labeled her "the best athlete ever." Over the years, every time Mr. Rooney saw Phyllis, he would break into a big smile, always greeting her with that title. Once, he had a pep talk with Kathleen and Phyllis to encourage them to take their studies seriously during the upcoming semester at Bethany College. He knew the two of them loved to have fun—so much so that he often jokingly accused them of thinking that every day was Christmas. (Truer words were never spoken.)

I myself experienced one of Mr. Rooney's teaching moments on a Sunday evening in October, 1974. I was driving Phyllis and Kathleen back to Bethany College in West Virginia and borrowed Mr. Rooney's car for the trip. Worried that my car would break down, Kathleen had urged me to use her dad's car, even though she always joked about "the piece of crap" he drove. His car wasn't fancy, but it definitely was a step up from my little 1970 Red Toyota; his car had no trouble getting up the hilly roads of West Virginia, while with my little Toyota I had to speed down hills to get a running start to get up the opposite hill.

I returned the car to Mr. Rooney's home when I returned to Pittsburgh, and he drove me to my home in Bethel Park. It was the first and last time I ever had one-on-one time with him. We were at the intersection of Washington Road and Conner Road, adjacent to the building where my dad's club, the Lebanon Lodge, used to be, when Mr. Rooney, bursting with enthusiasm, asked me, "Did you watch the Steelers game?"

I told him I had, and remarked on what a great game it had been. The Steelers had beaten their longtime rival, the Cleveland Browns, that afternoon, and it had been a close one.

Mr. Rooney then asked me, "How's Duquesne?"

I told him it was hard. I expected he would reply with words of encouragement, or even sympathy. But he startled me when instead he said emphatically, "It's supposed to be hard! All you're there for is to learn how to think!"

Mr. Rooney died on April 13, 2017. He left us with a final teaching moment in the form of a quote included in his obituary, which was published in *The New York Times* the next morning:

"Football and the Steelers have taught me lessons about perseverance, the belief in possibilities, the expansion of boundaries, the kindness of people and the unpredictability of life."

———

While I struggled in the early years of my CPA practice, and when I dealt with the many challenges I faced at the Fletcher School and in the startup years of the GPBF, I had many occasions to remember Mr. Rooney's words: *It's supposed to be hard!*

The hardest thing for the GPBF, like so many other charitable organizations that rely on public donations, is raising money. In the peace building field, what I describe as "getting beyond the metrics" is the major hurdle.

We invited two guests to attend our November 1, 2011, board meeting. We were just a little over a year old, very much in the formative stage. One of our guests had a philanthropic background; the other came from the banking industry. Their comments pertaining to how GPBF grantees measure and evaluate the outcome of their peace building work were telling.

The philanthropist commented, "It's a no-brainer that this work is beneficial."

The banker noted, "The GPBF should tell donors how success is measured."

Inevitably, when I give a presentation, I can always count on that million-dollar question. It comes in various forms: *How do you measure the outcome? How do you know it works? How do you know if the programs are successful? How do you know if it makes any difference?* This is a huge challenge for the GPBF, and in the peace building field in general. In our culture, there exists a strong scientific reliance on quantifiable data to measure outcomes, but a lot of the gains central to peace building are hard to quantify.

The lack of tangible, hard data is a real deterrent in attracting donor dollars. M. Scott Peck writes about this in his book *The Road Less Traveled*:

The use of measurement has enabled science to make enormous strides in the understanding of the material universe. But by virtue of its success, measurement has become a kind of scientific idol. The result is an attitude on the part of many scientists of not only skepticism but outright rejection of what cannot be measured. It is as if they were to say, 'What we cannot measure, we cannot know; there is no point in worrying about what we cannot know; therefore, what cannot be measured is unimportant and unworthy of our observation.' Because of this attitude many scientists excluded from their serious consideration all matters that are—or seem to be—intangible. Including, of course, the matter of God.

We cannot quantify how our human encounters, our human experiences, transform us. We must be open to the spirit, look for and welcome the spirit—the grace of God. We cannot measure that—and science cannot explain it either. That is more than science can provide.

The GPBF grantees are planting seeds that ripple out in unknown directions. Not expecting to get direct, concrete feedback on their actions, they know that it is the act of planting the seed that really matters. They do, however, have significant anecdotal evidence of the transformational experiences of their programs' participants. Take, for instance, Micah Hendler, a 2004 SOP Seed. Inspired by his camp experience, Micah founded the Jerusalem Youth Chorus (JYC) in 2012. A choral and dialogue program for Palestinian and Israeli youth in Jerusalem, JYC promotes a space for these young people from East and West Jerusalem to grow together in song and dialogue, giving its participants a voice.

And we know that when one mind is changed, when one heart is warmed, a ripple effect occurs. The work of a few affects the lives of many.

This is what the GPBF hangs its hat on—the ripple effect. Alexandrea Hollien, a Swiss writer, said, "It is like the rings in the water when you toss a pebble. At first the circles are very small, then they get larger, and finally they embrace the entire surface of the ocean."

———

CHAPTER TWENTY-FIVE

Do the Right Thing

"Keep true, never be ashamed of doing right; decide on what you think is right and stick to it."

—GEORGE ELIOT

When Sister John Ann encouraged me to always do the right thing in my life, she told me that it wasn't going to be easy. She was right. I have found that the richness in life is in the struggle as you find your voice, make your voice heard, and live into being true to yourself. This may take you to an uncomfortable or possibly scary place initially, but you will emerge from it with an authentic and empowered life full of passion, meaning, and purpose. This is the silver lining that comes with the inherent difficulty of doing the right thing.

I'm put in mind of a particularly harrowing life experience that nevertheless built my resources of inner strength and hope—just what I needed as I later set out on my Fletcher School and GPBF journey. It was a long legal battle that taught me to stick to what my heart told me was the right thing to do; and just as important, it gave me renewed confidence that kind people would emerge and help me along the way.

———

For a seven-year period before I started my own CPA practice, I held a Chief Financial Officer (CFO) position. This successful seven-year run came to a screeching halt on Friday, November 12, 1993, when my six-figure compensation package was annihilated. I was the sole income provider for my family, and this was a devastating economic blow. We went from a six-figure income to zero, overnight; we also lost our health insurance.

My employment was abruptly terminated because I had opposed the unlawful firing of a female employee (hereinafter, "the Abused") who had filed a formal written sexual-harassment complaint against the company. She showed great courage in filing her complaint, and she took on great risk, considering that she was a single parent supporting two daughters. I had first-hand knowledge of the history of the transgressions against her, and I knew that she had been terminated in retaliation, a great injustice. Besides that, her situation reminded me of my mother, who for many years had been the sole income provider for my family. For these reasons, I had a lot of empathy for the Abused and felt compelled to support her.

Two members of the management team (hereinafter, "the Betrayers") were responsible for the unlawful termination. They tried to disguise the reason for the termination by saying it was "a cost-cutting measure"—but as the company's CFO, I was supposed to initiate any such measures, and the Betrayers did not consult with me beforehand about this one. They announced the termination at a management meeting. I immediately opposed it, and the Betrayers became very angry at me, yelling at me as they attempted to defend their decision. Still, I wouldn't buy into it. I knew better ... and they knew it.

In retrospect, that was the beginning of the end of my employment there. Despite my objection, the Abused was fired, and she quickly filed a new sexual-harassment complaint with the Equal Employment Opportunity Commission (EEOC). After that, things got very tense for me at work. The Betrayers deliberately avoided me, and I was isolated. At the conclusion of a Board of Directors meeting, soon after the EEOC charge was filed, the Chairman of the board asked me to leave the meeting. I accidentally overheard the discussion that followed (my office was adjacent to the conference room), and was shocked to hear that it was about me! I couldn't hear every word, but in essence, the Betrayers told the board that I was supporting the Abused in her EEOC claim against the company, and persuaded the all-male board (hereinafter, "the Enablers") to go along with terminating my employment too.

I consulted with an attorney after overhearing that discussion, and he told me not to be surprised if I received a performance letter in the very near future, using "poor performance" as a rationale for terminating my employment. He went on to advise me that if my employers did that, it would be considered retaliation—in violation of Title VII of the Civil Rights Act of 1964—and I would be protected by the law. I thought, *Are they really that stupid?*—but I was relieved that at least the law was on my side.

Sure enough, within a week, the sham went down. I later deduced that the Betrayers had consulted with a law firm—I'll call the firm "the Dirty Rotten Scoundrels," or "the Scoundrels" for short—and together the Scoundrels and the Betrayers proceeded with their plan to terminate my employment due to poor performance, even though I'd received salary increases and bonuses consistently every year for the previous seven years.

On August 12, 1993, the Betrayers handed me a 90-day performance letter, obviously written by the Scoundrels, citing bogus defi-cient-performance issues. To make matters worse, they waited to give me the letter until the very end of the workday, as I was walking out the door—knowing that I was leaving the next morning for a family vacation in South Carolina. Bastards! On top of everything else, they wanted to ruin my vacation and inflict as much emotional distress on me as they could. I felt betrayed and hurt.

On the way home that evening, I was almost in a state of shock. They really had gone through with it, just as the attorney had predicted! It was hard to believe. But as my brain kicked into survival mode, I began to formulate a plan. *Enough of this bullshit!* I thought—now was the time in my life to go out on my own, start my own CPA practice, and determine my destiny. I'd often thought and talked about doing it; clearly, now was the time. I'd put my heart and soul into that job, and they'd betrayed me. I vowed to never let someone do this to my family and me, ever again.

I'll never forget how Phyllis reacted when I walked in the front door, pulled her aside into the dining room right in front of our grandfather clock, and told her the startling news. (Not wanting the kids to hear me, I whispered.) Her first words were, "What are we going to do?"—and at that moment, I had a flashback to when I was a young child, standing in my kitchen, and my Dad came home unexpectedly in the mid-morning to tell my mother that he'd been fired. My mother had said those same identical words: "What are we going to do?"

I tried to enjoy my vacation with my family as much as possible. Phyllis and I purposely didn't talk about the scary future. But my mind was in high gear as I formulated my game plan for the next 90 days and after. When I returned to work, the Betrayers greeted me with smirks on their faces. They seemed to enjoy the havoc they'd created for me—they were in retaliatory mode, with a vengeance. My attorney advised me to keep quiet: not to say a word, nor to take the bait as the Betrayers deliberately humiliated me and tried to provoke me into a confrontation. I felt like a boxer against the ropes, slightly slumped over and protecting my face and head as the Betrayers took turns pummeling me. I received a follow-up performance letter in September, another in October, and the final letter at the end of the day on Friday, November 12, 1993.

After my employment was terminated, I attempted to resolve the matter without going through drawn-out and expensive litigation. I already had an open EEOC claim pending—I'd immediately filed it after I received my first performance letter—and so I asked my attorney to request a severance package. I was hopeful, and in hindsight quite naïve, to make this request. The Betrayers' reply was cutthroat: they offered nothing.

I literally sobbed after I got off the phone with my attorney. Phyllis was on the floor below me and, hearing me sobbing, rushed upstairs to try to comfort me. She told me she'd never seen me so sad before. But it angered me too, because the Betrayers were deliberately trying to hurt me. They wanted me and my family to suffer; they wanted to silence my voice forever.

It soon became clear that my attorney lacked the interest and commitment to move forward. It was all just a transaction to him; the quick buck he made was all he'd wanted. So I fired him, then tried to work with the EEOC by myself for close to a year. The case went nowhere—there was no sense of urgency with the EEOC either. In the meantime I interviewed other attorneys, but none of them wanted to take on the Scoundrels. One predicted that the Scoundrels would live up to their reputation for a scorched-earth approach, and ruthlessly and deliberately destroy me at any cost whatsoever. Others told me that they would stall indefinitely in an attempt to wear me down. None of the attorneys I interviewed would take the case on a contingency basis; they didn't want to have any skin in the game. (At that time I didn't yet have any income from my newly founded CPA practice, so I couldn't afford their hourly fees and out-of-pocket expenses.) I was between a rock and a hard place—and I felt utterly alone.

Around that time, I remember taking a walk on a hot, sunny summer afternoon from my home to Vernridge Field, the field where I'd practiced football with my St. Anne School teammates some twenty-five years before. As I sat on the bleachers, I reminisced and reflected on the past. When I had played football there as a kid, on that same soil, I'd been innocent; life was simple. So much had changed over the years.

I prayed then, saying to God, "I never thought life was going to be this hard...please give me strength to get through this rough patch."

And then I remembered how The Image, my dad's dancehall, had been discriminated against in its first year of business. The local borough's politicians had enacted an anti-noise ordinance, and the District Magistrate had levied a fine against my father. My dad appealed the ruling to a higher court. On the day of the hearing, in the appellate judge's chambers, the judge lambasted the borough's solicitor, saying, "This ordinance should never have been enacted! It is blatant discrimination!" He then threw out the ordinance—and justice was served. My dad's voice, which had lain dormant for so many years, was finally heard. It was momentous. And the memory of it gave me hope that the justice system would work for me, and my voice too would eventually be heard.

In that hope, I pushed forward. I continued my search for an attorney to represent me—and miraculously, an angel entered my life. I felt the divine intervening when I first sat down and talked to this attorney, whom I will call the Heroine.

The Heroine worked with a mid-size law firm, and initially, she neither took my case nor turned it down. Most importantly, she spent time with me to talk it over. It was what I needed most—she listened to me when I thought I no longer had a voice. I met with her over the course of several months to keep her apprised of my pending EEOC case, and we built a professional relationship, and ultimately a lasting friendship, around trust and mutual respect. For the Heroine, my case wasn't just a transaction. She was able to see beyond herself to the bigger picture—the blatant discrimination and injustice of my former employers. Having faced discrimination in her own professional life and been forced to fight hard to rise to the top echelons of her law firm, she had fire in her belly, a fascination for the case, and great courage. And when the time came, she stepped up.

I received a subpoena from the Scoundrels to testify in a deposition in the Abused's federal sexual harassment lawsuit, and the Heroine agreed to represent me. The deposition fell on, of all days, a Valentine's Day. (There was certainly not a lot of love in the air that cold February evening.) Two attorneys representing the Abused also attended, along with one of the Betrayers and an attorney from the Scoundrels who reminded me of the Wicked Witch of the West in *The Wizard of Oz*. (I'll refer to her as "the Witch" hereinafter.) The Heroine had just given birth to a daughter, her third child, just a week before the deposition, so she asked to postpone—but the Witch, living up to her reputation, was unwilling to reschedule.

The rest of us were sitting and waiting in the conference room when the Witch and the Betrayer finally arrived and hurriedly sat down, directly across from me at the conference table. This was the first time I'd seen either of them for well over a year since my employment termination, and needless to say, it was quite awkward. But what struck me the most was that neither of them could make eye contact with me. They stared down at their documents, or at the table, the entire evening. To me, that was a stark display of their cowardice—but it didn't make the process any easier for me. This was the first of many depositions that I would have to testify in, and I was very nervous. I had all of the symptoms: the butterflies in my stomach, sweaty palms, racing heart, and dry mouth.

There was no friendly chitchat, no casual small talk. The Witch got right down to business, plopping a big stack of files onto the conference table and beginning her assault. Her first question pertained to my EEOC case, not the Abused's lawsuit, which caught me off-guard enough that I hesitated. The Witch pressured me, ordering me repeatedly, "Answer the question! Answer the question!" When I answered the question, my answer prompted the Witch to spout out an avalanche of hostile follow-up questions filled with ridicule and sarcasm, without giving me a chance to answer. At that point, the Heroine asked the court reporter to momentarily go off record—essentially to stop the deposition—then she pointed at the Witch and told her, "You need to be respectful to my client, or else this deposition is over." The Witch backed down, and the Heroine set the tone for the rest of the deposition. But that didn't prevent the Witch and the Abused's attorneys from screaming at each other throughout the remainder of it.

When it was done, the Heroine gave me a ride home. When we pulled into my snow-covered driveway, she turned to me and told me that she would take the case on a contingency and pay all of her out-of-pocket expenses herself. I could not thank her enough—and I still can't.

After that deposition, it only took five days for the Abused and the company to reach a settlement. Little did I know that *our* day in court would not come for five years. The Scoundrels lived up to their reputation: they stalled, delayed, and took the scorched-earth approach. It was like pulling teeth for us to obtain the documents we requested. In many instances, they refused to provide documents that we deemed critical; in others, the documents they did provide were heavily redacted.

But the Heroine was a real fighter. She persisted, remaining steadfast on my behalf—and ultimately the Scoundrels, at the behest of the Enablers and the Betrayers, made a huge error of judgement. In their quest to destroy me, they let their vengeance get the best of them—and they did something that, for the federal judge in the case, turned out to be the last straw.

It was late on a Friday afternoon when I received a call from an investigator from the Pennsylvania State Board of CPAs. He told me he was investigating a complaint filed by the Scoundrels, which requested that my CPA license be revoked. Stunned, I asked him what the nature of the complaint was. The investigator provided me with the details of the complaint, and asked me to respond to the allegations. I told him the truth—that the allegations were bogus and retaliatory—and the State Board of CPAs eventually dismissed the Scoundrels' complaint.

But their desperate and malicious act would come back to haunt them. The Heroine filed an amendment to our original federal complaint, spelling out the Scoundrels' ruthless retaliatory action. It was the epitome of their scorched-earth approach, she pointed out; their intent was to strip me of my CPA license and force me to close my practice, essentially destroying my livelihood. When my trial date finally came around, the federal judge scornfully pressured the Scoundrels to settle with me, citing the egregious action they'd taken against me with the State Board of CPAs. Reluctantly, they made me a settlement offer—what I'd originally requested as a severance, immediately after my termination five years earlier—and I accepted.

Although she never told me so, I felt that the Heroine was disappointed that we didn't pursue the trial. She'd worked hard, and was prepared for the fight. But I was deeply in debt, Phyllis and I were eager to end our five-year litigation nightmare, and in the end I just didn't want to take the risk. And though the ending was anticlimactic, I felt like a ton of weight had been lifted from my shoulders—and I must admit that I got a great deal of satisfaction when I saw the defeated faces of the Scoundrels and the Betrayers as they exited the judge's chambers.

———

The sham perpetrated by the Betrayers, the Enablers, and the Scoundrels really struck a chord with me, and has stuck with me ever since. It makes me furious when a person speaks in *spin*—in half-truths, or in the absence of truth (i.e., lies)—when information is twisted, or when people are cunning or deceitful. I lose trust and respect for people, and the so-called "leaders" of institutions (particularly government and churches), who operate in this manner.

Just speak the truth! Lay out the facts, good or bad. When our leaders deliver spin, it erodes our basic trust in them; it's upsetting and concerning. We must teach our children to know truth, live their lives with integrity, and always do the right thing—even if it is the hard choice. (It will be. You can count on that!)

Still, if you asked me if I'd go through that whole ordeal again, I would answer yes, definitely. It was a watershed moment in my life, a moment when I had to take a stand and confront lies and deceit. I had to fight the fight—to take on the big boys, even though they possessed a deep arsenal of weapons (resources and cash) to fight me. I couldn't walk away from it without having my voice heard, without having my day in court, without speaking truth to power. And its positive ending gave me hope in this world: hope that the truth, if you pursue it, will ultimately prevail.

I count my blessings, even to this day, that I had the Heroine by my side throughout that chapter in my life. She made a real difference; I couldn't have done it without her. She gets uncomfortable when I thank her, which happens every time I see her or speak with her over the phone. I always get choked up, with tears in my eyes. I can't help it.

The difficulties I experienced during that five-year lawsuit, and the sense of freedom I felt when it was over, instilled a new empathy in me for the injustice and suffering brought about by other types of discrimination around the world. This would influence me when I established the GPBF to give a voice to the oppressed, rectify injustice, and vigorously support nonviolent conflict resolution. Like so many of my experiences to that point, it became an important part of my life's purpose.

––––

In my essay for the Fletcher School application process, I wrote that I was increasingly focused on the exploration and discovery of ways I could make a difference in this world, find meaningful purpose in the second half of my life, fulfill a burning desire to make a mark and leave a legacy, and contribute to the greater good of the world. Richard Lieder's workshop at Omega, "Claiming your place at the fire: Living the second half of your life on purpose," undoubtedly influenced my thinking. You will most likely experience these same feelings at some point in your life, if you haven't already. As you have seen, my subsequent Fletcher School experience led me on the path to establish the GPBF and fulfill those aspirations. Accomplishing that, like my fight against the Betrayers, reinforced my belief that if you do the right thing for the right reasons, nothing can stop you.

Finding meaningful purpose may not be an easy path for you to take. You may have to change careers. You may have to be bold, follow your passion, and chart a path into the unknown. You may have to volunteer your time and talent without receiving monetary compensation. But in any case, it's worth it.

From the outset with the GPBF, I decided not to take any monetary compensation as its founder and executive director. I simply felt that it was the right thing to do ... and utter joy and happiness have been my reward. I've learned that such joy and happiness are derived—and perhaps *only* derived—by truly getting outside of yourself, by being altruistic, and by doing something meaningful to change the world.

―――――

CHAPTER TWENTY-SIX

The Power to Change the World

"Time," written by Angelo Mario Gabriele (Gabriel)

We should start early to cherish each new day,
And try to do something in some useful way,
To leave the world better than what we found,
To plant some seeds gladly in hearts to abound,
I know that I'm planning in my time to give,
Some small thing from my life to young hearts that live,
If even one portion grows fully and tall,
I'll know that my life here was good after all.

The air was crisp and the leaves were changing colors all around. I was immersed in work in my third-floor home office when I received a text message from Kristen, sent to our entire family: "There's an active shooter at a synagogue in Squirrel Hill [a Pittsburgh neighborhood]." Kristen, an elementary school teacher, was all too familiar with active-shooter drills and conducting lockdown drills in her classroom, and felt compelled to alert us.

The gunman killed eleven worshipers at the Tree of Life synagogue that morning. He had posted prolifically about his hatred of Jews and immigrants on social media leading up to the massacre. His posts celebrated the Holocaust and called for the eradication of Jews. To date, the shooting is the deadliest antisemitic attack in United States history.

Hatred drove that gunman to kill those innocent human beings that morning. Somewhere along the way in his life, he learned to hate.

Through my Fletcher School thesis research, I learned that prejudice and stereotyping are how the human brain works. Hatred, however, is learned. I often begin a GPBF presentation by asking attendees to raise their hands if they think they're prejudiced. Usually, no one will raise their hand. Unfortunately, whether we believe it or not, we are all prejudiced. Overcoming or even reducing prejudice and stereotyping are a challenge, because those things are part of the human condition. Our minds think with the aid of categories, and categories form the basis of normal prejudgment and prejudice alike.

The cognitive process of categorization classifies individuals into categories or groups—in essence, taking the individuality from individuals. Stereotyping and prejudice are a result of this cognitive process. Studies show that categorization begins in early childhood, possibly as early as four years of age.

My first memory of categorization comes from the early 1960s, when I was around six or seven years old and my mother and I boarded a bus near our home on Elderwood Drive in Bethel Park, on our way to downtown Pittsburgh. Noticing that all the black Americans were sitting at the back of the bus, I pointed to the back of the bus and asked my mother why this was so. She hastily grabbed my hand and told me to be quiet as we sat down in the front of the bus.

A subsequent memory of prejudice was born in the summer of 1963, when I was exposed to the racial tensions that were building in the United States. At the dinner table one evening, my dad expressed concern about a group of black teenagers that had shown up at the Lebanon Lodge the night before. He said that they hadn't danced that evening, but just stood along the periphery of the building in front of the windows, by themselves, set apart from the crowd. My dad seemed relieved that the black teenagers didn't interact with the white teenagers, and that no fistfights had occurred. This type of thinking was foreign to me: a person being seen and looked at differently, just because of the color of their skin. It didn't make sense.

This left a mark on me. Up to that point in my life, I'd never heard my parents say a word that would express any type of prejudice toward anyone. And as an adult, I now realize that my dad was merely expressing concern for his business: he was hoping that the underlying racial tensions that existed in our country at that time would not spill over and lead to violence and bad publicity for his teenage dance hall.

But it was a huge blessing that my parents didn't teach me to hate, period, and especially not to hate any other person because of their race or ethnicity. What I have come to learn is that this type of thinking, hatred, is taught, and that once it is taught, the likelihood of it passing from one generation to the next generation is very likely. It's very difficult to break that vicious cycle.

Reversing this vicious cycle is a tall order for the GPBF. But we are not alone. For the past decade, the GPBF has been providing support to programs at the grassroots community level that bring youth and children together, across differences, to learn, grow, and thrive, paving the way for a more peaceful future. As Shantideva, the 8th century Indian philosopher said, "How many malicious people can I kill? They are everywhere, and one can never come to an end of them. But if I kill hatred, I will overcome all of my enemies."

And in this journey, I have come to firmly believe that we as individuals, as ordinary citizens, have the power to change the world. It is within our grasp. All we must do is claim responsibility and realize that we have the freedom to do so. For my part, I didn't want to continue to hand over peace building responsibilities to the government or big organizations like the United Nations. Instead, I sought to become empowered to take my own path and establish a foundation to build sustainable peace. Through that process I came to believe, with Steve Jobs, that the ones who are crazy enough to think they can change the world, are the ones that do.

My hope now is that I can live a long life and amplify GPBF's voice by increasing awareness of youth and children's peace building programs operating under the Contact Theory; expand the GPBF's global grantee portfolio; stem the vicious cycle of hate passing from one generation to the next; bring more individuals into the fold who are willing to invest in building peace; and build a succession plan for the next generation to carry the torch. I pray, too, that Phyllis will be alongside me to the end of my journey.

On March 20, 2017, at the end of a presentation I made at the Mt. Lebanon Library entitled "Building Lasting Peace in Northern Ireland," an elderly woman handed me an affirming note while she was leaving. It read:

> "One person can change the world, and everyone should at least try."
> —John F. Kennedy

———

Acknowledgments

Many Acknowledgements sections I've seen appear almost as after-thoughts to the books they're part of: clichéd and cursory. I am deeply aware that my book is about a journey that could not have happened without others—people who helped me find my way, be myself, and be true to my voice—and so it is crucially important to me to thank them sincerely and authentically. It's just another of the many important ways we build community with one another in this life.

Firstly, this book wouldn't have come into being if it were not for all of the enormously talented and kind editors, writing coaches, and consultants who guided me on this four-year, 1,100-plus-hour writing journey. Much gratitude goes to:

Kelly Notaras, who gave me the inspiration and structure to write this book after I attended her five-day workshop at the Omega Institute in October 2019. Her book, *The Book You Were Born to Write*, turned out to be a treasure-chest resource.

Tia Meredith, who taught me to tap into and write in sensory detail.

Ben Leroy, who gave me critical big-picture feedback and helped me write my story more effectively by eliminating much detail.

Sara Henry, who provided me with the granular, hands-on assistance I needed as I paired down my manuscript.

Taylor Smith, a Fletcher School GMAP alumnus, who applied her journalism skills in helping me develop profiles for the book.

Jennifer Silva Redmond, who reinforced the need to show, rather than tell, my story.

James Carpenter, who, with the unique combination of an eye for detail and the ability to see the big picture, helped me see things I would never have seen.

The St. Anne School community was brought back to life in 1994 with our 25-year grade-school reunion. I am grateful for so many of my classmates who have since continued to help organize these heartwarming gatherings, which bring me home to my roots. These genuine friendships have endured the test of time, and I cherish them.

I am forever grateful to the Southminster Church community for nurturing my spiritual development. Their support after 9/11 will always be remembered, and their financial sponsorship and sincere words of encouragement helped me complete my degree at the Fletcher School.

Many thanks go to the Fletcher School, where I discovered meaningful purpose for the second half of my life. I am deeply indebted to Nicki Sass and Diana Chigas, both of whom played such special roles in making that happen.

The GPBF has been blessed over the past 13 years with many individuals who have contributed their time and talent to develop the organization, leading it from a startup to a full-fledged philanthropy. Thank you to Sarah Abboud, Amaka Azikiwe, Jessica Berns, Laura Boyd, Shannon Bruder, Gavin Byrum, Mardi Centinaro, Ed Cipriano, Katie Etzel Dailey, Chris Daley, Mark Etzel, Phyllis Etzel, Michael Fahey, Dana Fenner, Sonja Finn, Topher Hamblett, Bujar Hoxha, Doreen Hurley, Kristen Jenkins, Mayuresh Kulkani, Michael Kunz, Beth Kurcina, Ruth Lande, Yavor Lazarov, Linda and Chris Loewer, Steven Lord, Bill and Carole Markus, Kerry McCann, Caitlin Miller, Michael Minnock, Kristen Etzel Morley, Amy Mrazek, Carla Rosemarino, May Salameh, Angela Semple, Kendall Simon, Brad Steines, Taylor Smith, Judy Sutton, Scott Tully, Beatriz Vergara, and Sue Vodzak.

The GPBF is also most grateful to the PSFG team. Special thanks to Alex Toma, Rachel LaForgia, Cath Thompson, and Istra Fuhrmann, for always welcoming us with open arms. We are blessed to be associated with the PSFG's philanthropic organizations and individual philanthropists, whose daring ambition truly inspires me.

Our grantmaking has been made possible through generous grassroots donor support, for which I am eternally grateful. (We reached the $150,000 milestone in donations on December 31, 2023.) The GPBF's grantees, who are the catalysts and agents for change, motivate us to expand our global grantee portfolio, and we are honored to contribute to their life-changing work.

I was blessed to have known the ultimate volunteer role model, our family friend Mary Fahey, who is a real saint in my mind. Mary was a volunteer speech and forensics teacher at St. Anne School for forty years, and never took a cent for her work. She was ever so proud of her students and how they blossomed under her instruction and guidance, and shared with me many stories of how they had grown up and pursued fulfilling lives. Her volunteer vocation brought purpose and happiness to her life, and she continued teaching well into her late eighties until her deteriorating health forced her to retire. She died on October 3, 2011, at the age of ninety-four. I am forever grateful to her.

One of my PSFG colleagues, Milt Lauenstein, is another person I know who has dedicated the latter part of his life to making the world a better place. Born in 1926, Milt had a successful career as a businessman, but his path took a very different turn in 2001, when he made the decision to retire and refocus entirely on peace building. "I felt the world had been very good to me, and that it was my turn to give back," he says. Still active in his philanthropy at the age of 97, Milt is someone I look up to and aspire to emulate.

For many years I chased the dollars, thinking that I had to increase the GPBF's donation level to make an impact. Lisa Sabrkhani Maroney's new startup program showed me that I was wrong. Through her, I discovered that smaller grants have the potential to transform young people's lives, and that those little things will become big things.

As a music teacher at an elementary school near Orlando, Florida, Lisa took the extraordinary initiative to create her own peace-education curriculum through music. Her intention was to cultivate a safe and secure environment for students who came from diverse economic and cultural backgrounds and who had been exposed to tragic mass shootings, and to plant the seeds of peace in their hearts and minds. The GPBF provided the seed money to launch Lisa's program, the Sound of Peace, and has continued to fund subsequent programs she has created.

My hope is that Lisa's story will serve as a template for other teachers in the world to emulate. I'm thankful to her for showing us how uniquely positioned teachers are to make a significant impact in the world.

Kathleen Rooney's mother, Patricia Rooney, was a master at doing the "little things"—small actions that create significant long-term effects.

She cheered me on while I worked my way through college, at a time when she was also pursuing a degree. When Phyllis and I married and moved to Denver, I was surprised when we started receiving *The New York Times* every morning, seven days a week. It was a gift from Mrs. Rooney, and started me on the path of reading that newspaper every day—a habit I have kept for the past 46 years.

Over the decade after I launched the GPBF, Mrs. Rooney sent me notes of encouragement to show her support in what she called "the wonderful and important work you are doing." Even after her husband passed away, when Phyllis and I arrived at the funeral home to pay our respects she was eager to hear all about what we were doing at the GPBF.

Mrs. Rooney passed away on January 30, 2021. I remain grateful for her interest and encouragement.

My parents, Rita and Elmer "Etz" Etzel, gave me my solid foundation in life. Raising my own family has given me empathy for the sacrifices they made for me and my siblings. They truly gave it their all, and I am most thankful to them for it.

And I would be remiss if I didn't express my gratitude to my in-laws, Richard C. and Elizabeth V. McCloskey, as well. They are patient and principled people, and I'm grateful for their sage advice.

I have also been blessed by the love and support I've received from my children Kristen, Katie, and Mark, and I am happy to see that they are finding their own respective voices.

Finally, I am eternally grateful for my wife Phyllis. It wasn't a random thing when I met her 51 years ago on October 21, 1972; her steadfast love has been a gift from God, and for all of my adult life she's been at my side to hold my hand, guide and encourage me, and make me whole.

More About The Global Peace Building Foundation (GPBF)

GPBF has established its unique place in the peace and security grantmaking field through the following:

Grassroots Approach—GPBF supports peace building activities that operate at the local or community level. The key premise is that lasting peace can and must be built from the bottom up by ordinary citizens. We believe that power resides not just with high-level decision-makers, but at the grassroots level as well. Each individual can make a difference.

Contact Theory—GPBF operates under the Contact Theory, a central tenet of peace building based on the belief that separation and unfamiliarity between conflicting groups can, and often does, breed negative attitudes such as stereotyping and prejudice, which can potentially escalate into hostility and violence. The Contact Theory believes that these negative attitudes can be reduced by promoting contact and familiarity between conflicting groups.

Long-term focus and approach—As both a fundraiser and a grantmaker, GPBF is uniquely committed to long-term investment in the peace building process. Rather than following a short-term and quantitative results-driven approach, GPBF focuses on long-term goals, supported by qualitative results. GPBF realizes that it will take many generations to undo the hatred, fears, and violence that have been passed down from one generation to the next. Our aim is to break this cycle and contribute to the building of sustainable peace that all children deserve.

Innovative business model—GPBF continues to develop an innovative model that combines advocacy, due diligence, and Precision Micro-Granting ($500 to $1,000 grants earmarked for specific programs or projects) to increase awareness of the culture-transforming work currently underway among ordinary citizens. Our model also provides donors with an opportunity to create their own impact through financial contributions.

Efficient, low-cost operation—With low administrative costs and bylaws that prohibit the board of directors from receiving any compensation, GPBF allocates 99% of its annual budget toward core programs. We intentionally emphasize and encourage volunteerism in ordinary citizens, empowering them to think and act on both local and global scales. Thomas B. Etzel, Founder and Executive Director, has taken zero compensation since the organization's inception.

Commitment to attitudinal change—Governments sign treaties and aid organizations spend billions of dollars a year, but only *people can make peace*. The change in attitude and beliefs, which happens in the formative stage of a young person's life, creates the conditions necessary for youth to form lasting relationships built on mutual trust and respect. Amid complex and shifting landscapes, this trust is the bedrock for sustainable peace.

Operating without geographic limitations—This allows GPBF to adopt a pure approach when selecting grantees and carrying out our core programming. We support organizations that operate locally, regionally, nationally, and globally, so long as they can demonstrate a continuing commitment to our criteria, regardless of where their operational base is.

———

The GPBF performs a thorough due diligence process (conducting interviews, reviewing financial/tax data and organizational documents, and performing site visits) to ensure that our grant goes toward youth peace building efforts and meets these GPBF criteria: follow the

Contact Theory and include an underlying peace education curriculum.

GPBF grantees include:

Peace Players International (PPI) is a global organization that uses sports to unite and educate young people in divided communities. PPI operates under the premise that "children who play together can learn to live together." It is a great example of eliminating enemies by making them your friends. GPBF grants support PPI in Belfast, Northern Ireland, as they bring together Catholic and Protestant young people through their integrated basketball program.

Seeds of Peace (SOP) facilitates dialogue and interaction at their peace camp in Otisfield, Maine. A significant goal of SOP is to enable dialogue program participants to see the human face of their enemies, and from that experience build relationships based on mutual trust and respect. GPBF grants provide scholarships for Israeli and Palestinian youth.

Musicians without Borders (MWB) focuses on the power of music to build peace, connect people, empower musicians as social activists, and train local youth as changemakers. MWB creates one of the only opportunities in Mitrovica, Kosovo, for youth of different religions and ethnicities to interact. GPBF grants support the Mitrovica Rock School, which provides daily lessons and band coaching sessions to connect youth through weekly inter-ethnic workshops and its program for ethnically mixed bands.

Sterling Park Elementary School's music curriculum, developed by Lisa Sabrkhani Maroney, emphasizes diversity and tolerance through its *Sound of Peace* and *Music Explorers: The Road Less Traveled* programs. Students are exposed to different cultures through the lens of music and explore their differences and similarities together through various experiences and shared activities. Students are encouraged to explore their feelings and understandings of the world and are given a place to express their ideas. GPBF grants provided the organization with seed money to pay for music instruments.

Breaking Ground, operating in Cameroon, Africa, educates children and youth around non-violence and peaceful conflict resolution. GPBF grants help pay for extracurricular "Peace Club" dialogue programs. The clubs use theatrical sketches and dialogue to illustrate peaceful resolution to conflict, reduce tensions, and build shared identities, preparing citizens for reconciliation and sustainable peace.

Dancing Classrooms—Pittsburgh operates a 10-week social development program for fifth and eighth graders, focusing on ballroom dancing. Respect and compassion are the guiding principles of the program. The dancing helps break down social barriers between children, teaches them honor and respect, improves their self-confidence, and helps them communicate with, cooperate with, and accept others, even if they are different. GPBF grants support the "Colors of the Rainbow Spring Team Match," an exciting competition that showcases the skills of Dancing Classroom students.

Jerusalem Youth Chorus is a choral and dialogue program for Palestinian and Israeli youth in Jerusalem. Their mission is to provide a space for these young people from East and West Jerusalem to grow together in song and dialogue. Through the co-creation of music and the sharing of stories, they empower youth in Jerusalem with the responsibility to speak and sing their truth, encouraging them to become leaders in their communities and inspire singers and listeners around the world to work for peace, justice, inclusion, and equality.

A portion of the Author proceeds from this book has been donated to the GPBF.
To donate, visit www.globalpeacebuilding.org

Appendix A - Thesis Proposal

Topic: *Impact of Track Three diplomacy on peace building in conflict settings*

Context: *There are three Tracks of Unofficial Third-Party Intervention in conflict situations. Track One diplomacy is third-party processes run by an unofficial actor with official actors as the participants. Track Two diplomacy pertains to unofficial diplomatic processes, usually involving civil society elites. Track Three diplomacy is carried on at the grassroots and local level. This form of diplomacy is based on the belief that sustainable peace requires transformation, on a gradual basis, over a long period of time. The range of activities is broad. "In addition to dialogue, training, and other mediatory activities that bring people together across conflict lines, track-three interventions include psychological work to help communities deal with trauma that violent conflict has produced; joint social, sports, and arts events; joint business or economic projects; peace education; social mobilization; economic and social development projects that establish concrete incentives for peace; and work with the media, religious organizations, and other shapers of public opinion, among others."[1]*

Research Question: *Has Track Three diplomacy affected peace building outcomes in conflict settings, such as Northern Ireland and West Africa? If so, what is the effect, and can it be measured?*

Hypothesis: *Track Three diplomacy does have an impact on the peace building outcomes in conflict settings. This thesis will also determine which organizations have done it well, and why.*

Methodology: *Research of several case studies will be employed to compare and contrast example organizations. Some example case studies include the following:*

The American Ireland Fund (irlfunds.org/aif) is a non-profit entity that was founded more than a quarter-century ago. The organization has raised more than $300 million to support programs of peace and reconciliation, arts and culture, community development and education.

The International Negotiation and Conflict Resolution Club at the Fletcher School recently hosted the Foundation for West Africa (www.tfwa.org) to speak about the utility of radio as a mechanism for peace, accountability, and stability in West Africa. This organization targets West Africa's core needs: accountable governance, human rights, literacy, health care, and sustainable economic development.

Seeds of Peace (www.seedsofpeace.org) is dedicated to empowering young leaders from regions of conflict with the leadership skills required to advance reconciliation and coexistence. Seeds of Peace's internationally recognized program model begins at its summer camp in Maine and continues through programming in regions around the world with innovative initiatives in the form of conferences, regional workshops, educational and professional opportunities, and an adult educators program.

Footnotes
Chigas, Diana. 2007. "Capacities and Limits of NGOs as Conflict Managers," in Crocker, C., Hampson, F. and Aall, P. (eds.), Leashing the Dogs of War. *Washington, D.C.: U.S. Institute of Peace. 560.*

Appendix B - Thesis Bibliography

Afzali, Aneelah, and Laura Colleton. "A Survey of Coexistence Projects in Areas of Ethnic Conflict." In Chayes and Minow (eds.), *Imagine Coexistence*. San Francisco, CA: U.S. Jossey-Bass Books, 2003.

Allport, Gordon W. *The Nature of Prejudice,* Reading: MA: Addison-Wesley Publishing Company, 1954.

Anderson, Mary B., and Lara Olson. *Confronting War: Critical Lessons for Peace Practitioners,* Cambridge: MA: The Collaborative for Development Action, Inc., 2003.

Ashmore, Richard, Lee, Jussim, and David Wilder. *Social Identity, Intergroup Conflict, and Conflict Resolution,* New York, NY: U.S. Oxford Press, 2001.

Babbitt, Eileen. "Insights and Challenges." In Chayes and Minow (eds.), *Imagine Coexistence.* San Francisco, CA: U.S. Jossey-Bass Books, 2003.

Brewer, Marilynn B. "Ingroup Identification and Intergroup Conflict." In Ashmore, Jussim, and Wilder (eds.), *Social Identity, Intergroup Conflict, and Conflict Resolution,* New York, NY: U.S. Oxford Press, 2001.

Brewer, Marilynn B., and Samuel L. Gaertner. "Toward Reduction of Prejudice: Intergroup Contact and Social Categorization." In Brewer and Hewstone (eds.), *Self and Social Identity*, Malden, MA: U.S. Blackwell Publishing Ltd, 2004.

Chayes, Antonio, and Martha Mino. *Imagine Coexistence,* San Francisco: CA: U.S. Jossey-Bass Books, 2003.

Chigas, Diana. "Capacities and Limits of NGOs as Conflict Managers."

In Crocker, Hampson, and Aall (eds.), *Leashing the Dogs of War.* Washington, D.C.: U.S. Institute of Peace. 2007.

Chigas, Diana, and Brian Ganson. "Coexistence Efforts in Southeastern Europe." In Chayes and Minow (eds.), *Imagine Coexistence.* San Francisco, CA: U.S. Jossey-Bass Books, 2003.

Church, Cheyanne, and Mark M. Rogers. *Designing for Results: Integrating Monitoring and Evaluation in Conflict Transformation Programs.* Search for Common Ground: Washington, D.C., 2006.

Coser, Lewis A. *The Functions of Social Conflict,* New York, NY: The Free Press, 1956.

Diamond, Louise, and John McDonald. *Multi-Track Diplomacy: A Systems Approach to Peace,* 3d ed. West Hartford, Conn.: Kumarian Press, 1996.

Duckitt, John. "Prejudice and Intergroup Hostility." In Sears et al. (eds.), *Oxford Handbook of Political Psychology.* Oxford: Oxford University Press, 2003.

Eriksen, Thomas Hylland. "Ethnic Identity, National Identity, and Intergroup Conflict." In Ashmore, Jussim, and Wilder (eds.), *Social Identity, Intergroup Conflict, and Conflict Resolution,* New York, NY: U.S. Oxford Press, 2001.

Lederach, John Paul. *Building Peace: Sustainable Reconciliation in Divided Societies*, Washington, D.C.: United States Institute of Peace Press, 1997.

Minow, Martha. "Education for Coexistence." In Chayes and Minow (eds.), *Imagine Coexistence.* San Franciso, CA: U.S. Jossey-Bass Books, 2003.

Ogata, Sadako. "Imagining Coexistence in Conflict Communities." In Chayes and Minow (eds.), *Imagine Coexistence*. San Francisco, CA: U.S. Jossey-Bass Books, 2003.

Sluzki, Carlos E. "The Process Toward Reconciliation." In Chayes and Minow (eds.), *Imagine Coexistence*. San Francisco, CA: U.S. Jossey-Bass Books, 2003.

Sommers, Marc, and Elizabeth McClintock. "One Coexistence Strategy in Central Africa." In Chayes and Minow (eds.), *Imagine Coexistence*. San Francisco, CA: U.S. Jossey-Bass Books, 2003.

Zigby, John. "Moving Towards Understanding." *Executive Summary of On-Site Interviews Conducted at the Seeds of Peace International Camp in Maine during the Summer of 2003*. Report submitted to Seeds of Peace by Zogby International, July 26, 2004.

About The Author

Tom Etzel developed a vision for building peace on a global scale while he studied at the Fletcher School of Law and Diplomacy at Tufts University. His Fletcher School thesis formed the cornerstone for the Global Peace Building Foundation (GPBF), which he founded on September 11, 2010. He has served as the GPBF's executive director without compensation since its inception.

Tom holds a master of arts degree in international relations from the Fletcher School of Law and Diplomacy. He received his bachelor of arts degree in political science cum laude from Duquesne University.

Tom is a certified public accountant and author. He has been the principal of his own tax practice for the past 30 years. He currently resides in Pittsburgh, Pennsylvania, with his wife, Phyllis Etzel. Tom and Phyllis have three children, Kristen, Katie, and Mark; a son-in-law, Aaron; two daughters-in-law, Nikki and Katie; and six grandsons, Elliott, Sullivan, Gilmore, Dashal, Hobson Thomas, and Thatcher.

Made in United States
Cleveland, OH
19 January 2025

13301206R00142